For Creation's Sake

Books by Dieter T. Hessel

Social Ministry

A Social Action Primer

Reconciliation and Conflict: Church Controversy Over Social Involvement

Edited by Dieter T. Hessel

For Creation's Sake: Preaching, Ecology, and Justice

Social Themes of the Christian Year: A Commentary on the Lectionary

Maggie Kuhn on Aging

For Creation's Sake

Preaching, Ecology, and Justice

Edited by Dieter T. Hessel

The Geneva Press
Philadelphia

Copyright © 1985 The Geneva Press

Book design by Gene Harris

First edition

Published by The Geneva Press ®
Philadelphia, Pennsylvania

PRINTED IN THE UNITED STATES OF AMERICA

9 8 7 6 5 4 3 2 1

Library of Congress Cataloging in Publication Data

Main entry under title:

For creation's sake.

    Papers from the Institute for Pastors on Eco-Justice Preaching, held in Stony Point, N.Y., Feb. 14–16, 1984.
    Bibliography: p.
    1. Human ecology—Religious aspects—Christianity—Congresses. 2. Creation—Congresses. 3. Christianity and justice—Congresses. 4. Preaching—Congresses. I. Hessel, Dieter T. II. Institute for Pastors on Eco-Justice Preaching (1984 : Stony Point, N.Y.)
BT695.5.F67 1985   261.8′362   85–816
ISBN 0–664–24637–0 (pbk.)

To William E. Gibson and Earl Arnold
of the Eco-Justice Project
and their network of friends,
who are forerunners of a shalom future

Contents

Contributors

W. KENNETH CAUTHEN
John P. Crozer Griffith Professor of Theology
Colgate Rochester Divinity School/Bexley Hall/
Crozer Theological Seminary

JAMES A. FORBES
Associate Professor of Preaching
Union Theological Seminary, New York

WILLIAM E. GIBSON
Coordinator, Eco-Justice Project
Center for Religion, Ethics, and Social Policy
at Cornell University

NORMAN K. GOTTWALD
W. W. White Biblical Studies Professor
New York Theological Seminary

ELIZABETH DODSON GRAY
Co-Director, Bolton Institute for a Sustainable Future
Wellesley, Massachusetts

DIETER T. HESSEL
Associate for Social Education, Program Agency
Presbyterian Church (U.S.A.), New York

ROGER L. SHINN
Reinhold Niebuhr Professor of Social Ethics
Union Theological Seminary, New York

E. DAVID WILLIS
Charles Hodge Professor of Systematic Theology
Princeton Theological Seminary

Preface

Chapters 1 through 7 of this book were first presented during an Institute for Pastors on Eco-Justice Preaching convened at Stony Point, New York, February 14–16, 1984. A team of resource persons from leading theological seminaries and study centers brought to bear the insights of biblical studies, systematic theology, social ethics, homiletics, and cultural analysis in order to stimulate and strengthen preaching to deal with eco-justice issues. The presentations were revised for publication by the authors in the light of suggestions from other resource persons and discussions with the pastors who took part in the event.

Approximately thirty-five Baptist and Presbyterian pastors participated in this forty-eight-hour continuing-education event. They were brought together under the sponsorship of the Responsible Lifestyle Task Force of the Joint Strategy and Action Committee, with financial help from the two denominations just mentioned. Participants heard and discussed the papers. They also shared their experiences in grappling with eco-justice concerns through preaching. Each pastor was asked to bring a prepared sermon based on a text supplied by Institute leaders. Selected sermons were presented at the Institute and critiqued as models, but space does not permit their inclusion here. A set of questions we asked each other in analyzing eco-justice sermons is found in my concluding chapter.

A combination of ecology and social justice, "eco-justice" refers to the interlocking web of concern about the earth's carrying capacity, its ability to support the lives of its inhabitants and the human family's ability to live together in harmony. It highlights the interrelatedness of such pressing issues as world hunger and world peace, the energy crisis and unemployment, appropriate technology and good work, biblical stewardship and feminist consciousness, racial justice and pluralistic community, lifestyle choices in response to poverty and pollution. The historic questions wherein God speaks with loving justice are whether humans will permit each other to live and enjoy a fair share of the fruits of the earth, and whether human activity will respect the limits of the earth's ability to support the community of life into the future.

Preaching that seeks to communicate God's word for our time will reflect these concerns and will liberate the church to act on them. If preaching is to do that, new habits of thought are required even as old questions are reexamined: How can preaching for creation's sake achieve depth of focus and not merely create more guilt in the congregation? What is the good news concerning population growth on a planet with ecological limits? How does environmental responsibility enhance or curtail abundant life?

How can the poor and the unemployed obtain justice beyond the charity that church and society now offer? Is there a particular word of judgment and hope that must be spoken to the social system that creates poverty and brutalizes nature? What is the divine Yes along with the No to modern society? Is there a uniquely Christian word to be spoken on behalf of nonhuman creatures threatened by the impact of human activity? What are appropriate human aspirations consistent with both contemporary knowledge and the timeless call to "seek first God's kingdom and justice"? Such are the questions addressed in the following chapters.

Special thanks are due to three persons for their staff work on this project: Earl Arnold, Associate Coordinator of the Eco-Justice Project at Cornell University, Ithaca, New York; Owen Owens, National Ministries staff, American Baptist Churches, Valley Forge, Pennsylvania; and John DeBoer, Executive Director, Joint Strategy and Action Committee, New York, New York. I am also grateful for the time and talent invested by the participants in the Preaching Institute and the coauthors of this book.

Dieter T. Hessel

Advent, 1984

1

Eco-Justice: New Perspective for a Time of Turning

William E. Gibson

I. Eco-Justice as a Biblical Theme

The Sovereign God is good to all,
    and has compassion over all creation. . . .
The Lord upholds all who are falling,
    and raises up all who are bowed down.
The eyes of all look to you,
    and you give them their food in due season.
You open your hand,
    and satisfy the desire of every living thing.
              (Ps. 145:9, 14–16, paraphrase)

The pastures of the wilderness drip,
    the hills gird themselves with joy,
the meadows clothe themselves with flocks,
the valleys deck themselves with grain,
they shout and sing together for joy.
              (Psalm 65:12f., paraphrase)

If you want to know what eco-justice is, read the book of Psalms. The dual theme of justice in the social order and integrity in the natural order is pervasive and prominent. The psalms are in large part a celebration of the interrelationships, the interaction, the mutuality, the organic oneness and wholeness of all that is—the Creator and the creation, human and nonhuman.

Millennia before there was any formal science of ecology, the psalmists, and indeed the biblical writers generally, were implicit ecologists, just as they were explicit champions of justice. Ecology is the study of an organism's relations with its environment. The psalmists believed that every part of creation was related to the rest and that the Creator continued to delight in all the created world and continued actively to care for the whole and its parts. They believed also that the goodness of God to all meant not only sustenance and protection but also restoration. Raising up those who were bowed down included raising up those who had been knocked down and held down. The Creator and the Deliverer were the same God. And if the victims to be delivered were most explicitly the human victims of greed, oppression, and violence, the realm of nature shared the agony of the victims, suffered again when judgment was executed upon the oppressors, and rejoiced in the restoration to peace, justice, and wholeness.

Nature, as viewed and personified by the psalmists, rejoices when the intention of the Creator is carried out, whether this is before there is any need for deliverance or after it has taken place. And the intention is health, fullness, mutuality, community, the satisfaction of the appropriate desire of every living thing. Justice itself is an ecological phenomenon, impossible without the proper maintenance of organic relationships. The processes of nature, employed and enhanced through human labor, provide human sustenance. But nature rejoices in those very processes; and nature's value and goodness as God's creation is prior to and extends beyond its usefulness to humans. Therefore, "the hills gird themselves with joy," while "the meadows clothe themselves with flocks" and "the valleys deck themselves with grain"; "they shout and sing together for joy" (Psalm 65:12–13).

II. Ecology Crisis as a New Fact of Our Time

No one today suggests that the strip-mined hills of West Virginia are girding themselves with joy; or that the river basins of the United States, carrying some four billion tons of topsoil to the sea each year, are celebrating the pollution of the water and the loss of the land's fertility; or that the acidified lakes of the Adirondacks are rejoicing in the death of the fish.

Concern about ecology in our time arises out of the realization that nature places limits upon human behavior. The limits were always there, written into the natural order as God created it. But the recognition of those limits is a distinctly contemporary occurrence, coming after several centuries of distinctly modern disregard for limits. The limits have become apparent as never before in history precisely because they were disregarded until the global consequences of disregard became unmistakable. This is not to say that there were no cases of serious ecological deterioration from human pressures until modern times, but they were strictly local or regional in scope. Ancient writers in China and in Greece expressed concern about the destruction of habitat by overgrazing and deforestation. In today's interdependent world the appearance of limits is a global phenomenon. The scope and speed of deterioration have been vastly extended. While of course the situation varies greatly from place to place, the problems of pollution, overpopulation, ecosystem instability, depletion of nonrenewable resources, degradation of renewable resources, and the looming of scarcities that neither market mechanisms nor technological fixes can overcome, all belong to what the Club of Rome calls "the world problematique." At issue here are the carrying capacity of planet earth and the quality of life for all its inhabitants.

This ecology crisis has come upon the world with relative suddenness and abruptness. It comes as the direct consequence of the concerted and systematic efforts by humankind in the modern era to dominate nature and bend it to the human will—the will not only to survive and multiply but also to banish the ancient insecurities and to achieve a boundless material abundance. It comes because these efforts succeeded spectacularly for a large minority of the people of the planet. In the Western world, then in Japan, and now to varying degrees in the so-called developing countries, science and technology have revolutionized industry, agriculture, and medicine. The life span of people in the developed world has doubled; the carrying capacity of earth has expanded enormously; and a life-style of big consumption and great mobility has become normative in the developed countries, while desired everywhere. And yet these "successes" constitute crisis, for they are ecologically unsustainable.

The abundance made real by science and technology and by the liberal[1] political and economic institutions of the modern era has never been shared as equitably as it might have been and ought to have been. In our own society an unconscionable amount of unnecessary poverty and misery has been tolerated, and indeed not just tolerated but systematically perpetuated by the ruling class as instrumental to its own excessive affluence. Internationally, poverty continues as the lot of the vast majority in the less developed components of the global system. The shame attached to the successful application of human ingenuity to the increase of production has been the inattention to, and in large part the deliberate denial of, the imperatives of distributive justice.

Nevertheless, modern civilization is distinguished by the reality of material abundance and the generally widespread participation in this abundance that prevails in the advanced industrial nations. The past three centuries, writes William Ophuls in a book entitled *Ecology and the Politics of Scarcity,* "have been an era of abnormal abundance, which has shaped all our attitudes and institutions."[2] He points out that John Locke, Adam Smith, and Karl Marx all shared the assumption that there would always be *more:* more land—at least in the New World and other places—to be explored and exploited, more mineral wealth to be dug out of the ground, more technique to make the most of these resources, and, if not more air and more water, at least plenty of these "free" reservoirs for absorbing the waste products of more industry. "Thus," says Ophuls, "virtually all the philosophies, values, and institutions typical of modern society are the luxuriant fruit of an era of apparently endless abundance." [3]

The ecology crisis, therefore, does not just come as a warning that pollution can be unhealthy or that disamenities will accompany overcrowding unless population growth is checked. It does not tell us simply to install more antipollution devices and distribute more birth control pills and let everything go on otherwise just as before. The ecology crisis presents a fundamental challenge to the assumptions and expectations most characteristic of our culture. As such, it is the great new fact of our time. It tells us that there are limits and scarcities to be reckoned with and respected, that production which uses up ever greater quantities of the world's finite supplies of fossil fuels and nonfuel minerals destroys the capital necessary for its own continuation, and that the same science, technology, and industry which have achieved the enlargement of the earth's carrying capacity will cause its contraction if they continue to overstrain the ecological foundation of economics.

In the heady times of modern scientific-technological triumphalism the implicit ecological wisdom of the biblical authors was overwhelmed and forgotten. The biblical idea of human dominion over the nonhuman creatures (Genesis 1:26–28) was wrenched away from the biblical context, so that this dominion, intended to be a dominion of loving and careful stewardship, became a dominion of ruthless mastery. To the human victims of greed, oppression, and violence, whose deliverance is God's work in the world, it becomes necessary now to add the nonhuman victims, the extinguished and endangered species, the strip-mined hills, the eroded croplands, the polluted rivers, the acidified lakes, the meadows and valleys that no longer sing for joy. Nature itself has become co-victim with the poor.

Perhaps the conquerors of the wilderness, the pioneers

of industry, the American "robber barons" of the nine-teenth century, the promoters of mechanized chemical agriculture, the real estate developers, and the heads of the multinational corporations did not know that their short-term triumphs could turn into long-term disasters, that nature's submission to their demands would lead in the end to nature's retaliation against its abusers. But they cannot be excused altogether for their lack of reverence and respect for God's creation, their perversion of the role of the steward. It is not fitting for us, however, to deny our own benefit from the human achievement in overcoming human want. Nor should we deny the positive moral dimension of that achievement, ambiguous though it has become.

Suddenly for us the situation is radically and unalterably changed. We can see the folly of trying to dominate nature without caring about it, the hubris of forgetting that we are part of nature. The evidence of limits is massive[4] and shows us how far we have departed from the biblical norm of a sustenance-giving but harmonious and responsible human relationship with the rest of God's creation. The Creator calls us to make science and technology sub-servient to that norm, as we look now at the creation in a radically new way that is nevertheless akin to a much older way. We have been warned, and we must learn what the ancient task of stewardship means in a time of ecological peril and scarcity for which there is no precedent.

III. Eco-Justice as the Connecting of Two Concerns

In 1972 the United Nations sponsored an International Conference on the Human Environment in Stockholm. The countries that sent delegations contained over 90 percent of the world's people. This event, together with the numerous nongovernmental gatherings surrounding it, was a landmark occasion signaling the new recognition around the world that human exploitation of the biosphere was cause for serious concern.

The Stockholm meetings, however, were notable also as an early and stormy confrontation between the environmentalists from the rich industrialized nations, on the one hand, and the representatives of poor nations, together with a variety of advocates for the poor and the oppressed, on the other. The arguments by the first group for limiting economic growth for the sake of environmental protection and resource conservation were received by the second group as bad news indeed. The latter quite correctly perceived that under the existing structures of power, patterns of distribution, and operating procedures in the international economic order a slowdown or cessation of economic growth would arrest badly needed development in the Third World and freeze the prevailing patterns of inequality or even make them worse. The critics of growth, whose countries had already arrived at a high level of consumption and comfort, were accused of wanting to pull the ladder of progress up and away from the poor, thus condemning the impoverished to continuing poverty.

The critics of the environmentalists (one might say the critics of the critics of growth) were not impressed by the limits-to-growth thesis. According to that thesis, the continuing exponential growth of industry and population would lead in the course of the next century to a situation in which continued growth would become quite literally impossible. Both population and industrial production would overshoot the bounds imposed by the earth's resources and systems. Following overshoot would come collapse, that is, a precipitous drop in industrial and probably also in agricultural production, and a rapid drop in population due to a soaring death rate. However, the advocates for the poor would not buy the argument. It should be quickly noted that very few people of power in industry or government in rich nations have bought it either. I think in both cases the argument has been rejected not because it lacks sufficient evidence but because it is disliked. It comes as bad news to both rich and poor, though their reasons are not the same.

People who are desperate for bread, or for a job, or for a return on a crop big enough to pay a debt and avoid foreclosure on a small piece of land, understandably do not worry about auto emissions or acid rain. Nor will they give much thought to the possibility of overshoot and collapse sometime after the year 2000. But then all of us who care about justice must refuse to allow the ecology crisis, with its warning to alter present trends while there still is time, to be used as a rationalization for perpetuating existing inequities, either in this country or on the international plane.

Writing in 1970, almost two years before the Stockholm conference but after the first Earth Day in the United States, Norman Faramelli addressed the dilemma of those who would at the same time care for the earth and do justice to the poor. In an article entitled "Ecological Responsibility and Economic Justice" he observed that "an increasing Gross National Product (GNP) has functioned in American society like a God-concept does in a religious society."[5] This indicates what anyone will encounter who suggests that we can get at the root causes of the ecology crisis only by curtailing the consumption of fuel and material in our economy.

> More growth means more jobs for all (especially the poor and middle income groups) and more public funds available to finance welfare programs (i.e., without further tax increases). We are addicted to the "trickle down theory," i.e., everyone must receive more if the poor are to receive more. That this theory has not been fully effective in ending poverty is irrelevant; it has worked in part. The poor may not have been helped appreciably by economic growth, but they certainly will suffer acutely if the growth rate declines.[6]

Despite this dilemma, Faramelli insisted that "to choose [to work for] ecology instead of [against] poverty, or vice versa, is to make a bad choice." [7] We have to choose both, but can we? Will we not be hopelessly at cross-purposes with ourselves? Faramelli plunged on to suggest very briefly a hard way out: a redistribution of national income, an adequate guaranteed annual income for all, and a change of life-style by affluent Americans in the direction of less consumption and more sharing.[8]

At the beginning of the 1970s the Board of National Ministries of the American Baptist Churches, under the leadership of Jitsuo Morikawa, was engaged in a three-year strategic planning process. Those were the years when the social action dynamics of the 1960s, focused on civil rights and against the war in Vietnam, continued strong, though some activists were beginning to grow weary from running up against entrenched resistance and stolid indifference to their objectives. They were also the years of the first cresting of the environmental movement, as manifested in the 1970 Earth Day, the 1972 Stockholm conference, and the publication of the report to the Club of Rome on the MIT-based computer projections of the global future under the title *The Limits to Growth*.[9] Some black leaders and other social activists were complaining that the environmental movement was a cop-out from the struggle for justice.

In the context of this convergence of two movements, the American Baptist strategic planners embraced the basic goals of both. A member of the staff, Richard Jones, now Secretary of the Board, coined the term "eco-justice" to make the connection of ecology with justice. The term became the title of a pamphlet written by Owen Owens that looked at both concerns from a biblical perspective and related them to the responsibility of Christians to shape the future.

> If we change our ways, we need not bring down upon ourselves atomic war, starvation, or other calamities. We dare to hope such change is possible. We dare to believe we humans can use our power rightly. Our generation can leave nature a little

more whole than when the pioneers first touched the wilderness. We can leave society more fair and equitable than the one we were born into. Humanity and nature can come together in eco-justice. Eco-justice means joining together concerns for ecology and justice.[10]

The pamphlet did not mention the controversy around the idea of limits to growth. It did define stewardship as "right management, particularly of economic life" and stated that a good steward "works to see that available goods and resources are distributed justly." The Board, meanwhile, decided to concentrate its efforts in the area of eco-justice in "the cultural or value-forming arena (the schools, the media, etc.) rather than in the economic or political arenas, . . . contending that no change will occur unless the value-forming institutions come to a new understanding of human life."[11]

The medicine prescribed by Norman Faramelli in 1970, for simultaneously curtailing the growth that was ecologically destructive and doing justice to the poor despite the limiting of growth, was much too strong for widespread acceptance. It was generally not very palatable to church people; it was anathema to economists, business executives, and labor leaders, and quite unthinkable for politicians. The American Baptist Board can hardly be faulted for contending that before such momentous changes in American political economy and culture could occur, the values of the American people would have to change. Still, if Faramelli's prescription was too strong, the Baptist espousal of eco-justice was a little pallid. A step in the right direction, it was not calculated to disturb anybody. The typical church member could easily pass over references to a just distribution and a "new understanding of human life" without realizing how very different that understanding would have to be to make meaningful and acceptable the sacrifice of income or the reduction of consumption that might be required of him or her in making distribution just.

The trouble is that eco-justice as concept or practice is bound to be disturbing if it keeps people from copping out on one side or the other. In our culture there is no simple and easy short-run reconciliation of ecological responsibility and economic justice.

IV. A Necessary New Perspective

In the slightly longer run there cannot possibly be any serious commitment to economic justice that is not inclusive of ecological responsibility. The short-run reconciliation is difficult because it violates the most deep-seated assumptions of our economy and our culture. But without ecological responsibility, achievements in behalf of justice can only be short-lived; that kind of "progress" in the present denies justice to the future.

Eco-justice, then, is the well-being of humankind—all humankind—on a thriving earth. It is acceptance of the truth that only on a thriving earth is human well-being possible—an earth productive of sufficient food, with water fit for all to drink, air fit to breathe, forests kept replenished, renewable resources continuously renewed, nonrenewable resources used as sparingly as possible so that they will be available for their most important uses as long as possible or until a renewable alternative can be utilized. On a thriving earth, human well-being is nurtured not only by the provision of these material necessities but also by a way of living within the natural order that is *fitting:* respectful of the integrity of natural systems and of the worth of nonhuman creatures, appreciative of the beauty and the mystery of the world of nature.

Humans cannot live in the world without altering their environment and making creative use of what it provides for their sustenance and enjoyment. But biblical themes of eco-justice combine with the warnings of the ecology crisis to insist that human interventions must be caring and careful. A thriving earth is not conquered but cared for.

Beyond our own needs are those of the generations to

come. The concept of justice must surely encompass their claims to sufficient sustenance on a thriving planet. But even that concept is not large enough. The earth has its own claims; it is not *only* a source of sustenance and enjoyment for human beings. Its integrity is to be respected not only because the protection of that integrity serves the self-interest of the human species, but because the whole creation is good and every part of it counts for something in its own right. God made it good; it has value to God; it makes a rightful claim on us. It still belongs to God, who never gave it away; we are permitted to take sustenance from it; we are entrusted with its care. The claim of the nonhuman to be respected and cared about, which is like the claim of every human neighbor near and distant, is ultimately the claim of God.

> For every beast of the forest is mine,
>   the cattle on a thousand hills.
> I know all the birds of the air,
>   and all that moves in the field is mine. . . .
> For the world and all that is in it is mine.
>   (Psalm 50:11–12)

Justice encompasses the obligations of stewardship. Justice on God's good earth is always eco-justice.

Nevertheless, it is very hard in the modern era to keep defining and practicing justice as eco-justice—to hold together our concern for people and our concern for nature. The nub of justice for people today is the access by all to the goods and services that they require for sustenance and fulfillment. In our society that access depends on having money, and money is obtained by working, and work for most people means holding down a job. But there are not enough jobs to go around, and some jobs that people do hold do not pay sufficient income. The most important feature, the sine qua non, of a society structured for justice is full employment—a job with sufficient pay for everyone who needs it—plus sufficient income maintenance for people who are not able to take a job.

The overriding issue for eco-justice in the last two decades of this century is whether full employment can be combined with ecological responsibility. And the answer is *no* if full employment can only be achieved through energy-intensive, resource-intensive, environmentally ruinous growth in the economy, determined by what is profitable for those who provide jobs, and entailing the production of a whole host of things that have little or nothing to do with sustenance and fulfillment. Republicans, Democrats, and most varieties of socialists, together with all the capitalists and most of the workers, still assume that the key to economic prosperity and economic justice is indiscriminate growth, the production of anything and everything that will sell. It has become increasingly difficult to generate enough growth for anything close to full employment. Nobody knows how to achieve it anymore. Still, nobody prominent in public life talks about full employment without growth or about the income redistribution, life-style simplification, national planning, and decentralized implementation that would be required to make it work.[12] We are engaged in a futile effort to achieve economic justice by means of an obsolete system that is unconscionably wasteful, unsatisfying to most workers, and ultimately suicidal.

And so it will be till we learn to look at the world in a whole new way. Eco-justice pushes us to the formation of a new social paradigm,[13] a new set of assumptions, standards, values, and habits appropriate to a new era in the history of the world, an era in which men and women come to terms, not only with the ancient imperatives of justice in the human family but also with the lessons of biblical faith and the ecology crisis—that the planet is finite and that justice must be eco-justice.

In the new paradigm the expectation of unlimited material "progress" and ever-increasing consumption will give way to a norm of sufficiency, enough without excess. The ever greater demand upon finite resources will give way to careful frugality and a transition to dependence on resources that are continuously renewed. The domination of nature will turn back into stewardship, respectful care, interacting with nature, and drawing sustenance from it according to a norm of sustainability. Competition and consumerism as means of establishing self-identity and gaining social esteem will give way to cooperation and the enjoyment of community. Work will be geared toward real needs, aesthetic and spiritual as well as material, so that it can be good work, expressing the talents of the worker and enriching the life of the community.

Eco-justice is, I believe, a necessary perspective for viewing creation at a momentous turning point in this world's history. It is a perspective for understanding what is happening and for envisioning and achieving an eco-just future. It is a perspective rooted in biblical faith that generates humility in the face of the realization of the harm that human beings in pride and greed and careless-ness have done to the planet and to their human neigh-bors. But it also generates hope from the realization that God is involved with us in the dangers, judgments, chal-lenges, and new possibilities of this time of turning.

V. A Perspective with Consequences

When the eco-justice perspective is communicated ef-fectively to Christian people who, nurtured by biblical preaching, know themselves to be actors in the ongoing drama of creation, desecration, and deliverance, it trans-forms the concept and the practice of Christian faithful-ness. The hearer knows that now, in this world and in this momentous time of turning, she or he either does or does not prove faithful.

For biblical people today faithfulness consists in *a style of life that fits a world imperiled.* The planet groans under the excessive demand by modern industrialism and consumer-ism for the comfort and indulgence of the dominant minority of humankind, even as the dominated majority groan under the frustration and misery of their ineffective demand for sufficient sustenance. In this context the shaping of a life-style that *fits* occurs only as citizens and societies begin to do what modern economists dismiss out of hand as impossible: to discriminate between the human wants that are needful and fulfilling and those that are unnecessary and excessive.

Therefore, when eco-justice preaching gets through to the typical "rich Christian"[14] in an American mainline congregation, that person's life-style will begin to change: away from a standard of consumption determined by what can be afforded, toward one based on a conscientious conception of enough.

We define life-style much too narrowly, however, if we think only of consumption and conservation. The eco-justice perspective requires the same typical American Christian to change in another way: away from careless, uncritical enjoyment of the benefits of political and economic arrangements that are unjust and unsustainable, toward democratic political advocacy and action in behalf of policies designed to further equity of distribution in the present, while protecting the ecological basis for sufficient sustenance in the future. This person will become less careless, less demanding, less wasteful in drawing upon the good things of God's creation, but at the same time more involved, more active, more political in seeking more of those good things for people who do not have enough. The eco-just life-style moves toward sufficiency by synchronizing careful habits of consumption with bold efforts to effect systemic change.

The eco-just life-style moves also toward community: away from the competitive individualism that maximizes one's own gain and causes another's loss, and toward cooperative, mutually supportive work and play. With less strain upon natural and social systems, there is more joy, more wholeness, more friendship, and more protection from hunger and hazard.

And so . . .

A young couple with an income sufficient to let them be

upwardly mobile decide not to go into debt for a house in the suburb but to stay in the city close to their friends. They buy a duplex house, adequate but not fancy, and invite another family to take the second apartment at a rental kept low so that they can afford to accept. The two families work together on painting and repairing. They share child care, enjoy a weekly meal together, and form a prayer group with a third couple. Their savings on housing give them a more secure position for facing the uncertainties and contingencies of raising children in troubled times. They can and do continue to give generously to their church and to various organizations that address human needs and the issues of eco-justice.

A young man with a "promising" position in computer programming with a large corporation finds that his work is not satisfying, because it does not meet the criteria of eco-justice for "good work." He leaves the job, moves back to the city where he used to live, and joins some friends in forming an intentional living community. He does not seek a paying job for a year or so but takes on gardening and other tasks for the intentional community, gets active in a church and becomes an adviser to the youth group, enjoys new and deepening relationships, and thinks carefully about what he wants to do. He decides to find a half-time position that will utilize his computer skills and permit him to devote the rest of his work time to volunteer projects that help people and foster eco-justice.

A physicist leaves a prestigious research institute because he can no longer engage in research in that place with integrity. The research projects must be designed to "succeed," because if too risky they will not get funded. The more important avenues of investigation are not pursued. The physicist forms his own small business for custom design of software. He enjoys serving other small businesses and appreciates the personal kind of service they give him. He becomes their advocate in the face of the encroachment of "superstores." He makes much less money than before but derives much more pleasure from making it. In his spare time he, with a partner, recycles houses—fixes them up and makes them available to people who otherwise could not afford a place so good.

These people have made the connection between the biblical story and the eco-justice perspective. Many more examples might be given—about people who have found new wholeness by nurturing, and being nurtured by, the land[15]; people who have become politically active in ways that seek to break out of the impasse that keeps the established parties from being relevant to the imperative of full employment combined with ecological responsibility; people who have learned, stuck with, and come to enjoy the tough, sometimes exciting, often tedious tasks of organizing for the nuclear freeze, for cleanup of the environment, for the unionization of underpaid and unappreciated workers, for peace with justice in Central America, for legislative advocacy to overcome world hunger, malnutrition, and cropland deterioration.

The eco-justice perspective indeed has consequences for Christian faithfulness in our time—and hence, in ways that can only partially be observed, making this time of turning a transformation in the direction of the justice, the eco-justice, that God seeks to bring. By no means are all the people in the pews ready for eco-justice preaching. To the extent that it is heard it will generate resistance as well as acceptance. But the preacher, whose own faithfulness is at stake, may discover that the perspective is not optional.

2

The Biblical Mandate for Eco-Justice Action

Norman K. Gottwald

There can be no doubt that the Bible expresses fundamental "concerns" about eco-justice. But do these concerns
gather and focus in a way that forms a *mandate,* an
authoritative command or instruction to do something?
How specific is the mandate? How do we negotiate between
widely separated biblical and contemporary worlds? What
is the role of the church in carrying out the mandate? What
is the place of preaching within the church's role?

Whether and how we translate biblical eco-justice concerns into mandates depends critically on our hermeneutical understanding, how we read biblical texts in the context
of their times and how we read ourselves in our times.
Ancient and modern texts come together in a fashion
which has been called "a fusion of horizons"[1] and in a
process which is called "hermeneutical circulation."[2] We
are always moving in dialectical fashion from our complex
present into a complex past and back again. Our basic
placement is present, but we come to a fuller grasp of the
present by "distancing" ourselves from a locked-in situation through critical engagement with biblical texts and
societies. In the profound differences and deep strands of
connection between the two times and texts we are led back
into our situation with perspective and with fresh possibilities and resources. Both the Bible and our situation must
thus become "strange" to us before they can become
"familiar," recognizable as our story and our destiny.

Let me first lay out some aspects of this fusion of horizons within a process of hermeneutical circulation. Then I shall speak of a central focus and structure of biblical society and religion which may inform all our eco-justice concerns.

I. The Hermeneutics of the Fusion of Biblical and Contemporary Horizons

The Bible Is Never Absent from Our Horizon

As Christian Westerners we carry the Bible in our common culture and our individual hearts and heads. We have a predisposition to think and evaluate biblically. The question is not really, "How shall we bring the Bible into treatment of this problem?," but rather, "How has the Bible all along, consciously or unconsciously, been shaping our perception of the problem?"[3]

The Bible Is Not Sufficient to Our Horizon

The Bible does not give a mandate of such totality of coverage and specificity of detail that it alone or primarily enables us to understand and respond in our setting. This is for two reasons. The most obvious reason is that our horizon is different from the Bible's in the sense that ours is a more complex society with new difficulties and opportunities. But there is a more fundamental reason for the insufficiency of the Bible to our time. All human action, however continuous with tradition and precedent, is fresh action. We take an action, and nearly always we could have taken some other action. Life has openness and indeterminacy within limits that are only found out by exercising our freedom. So we must know many other things over and above the Bible, and we show that we understand the biblical conception of freedom under God precisely when we own our own insight and courage and do what we must do.

Both Horizons Must Be Critically Re-visioned

In the hermeneutical circulation we have only provisional resting places, because again and again we must reassess the biblical texts in their times and our place in our times. Fresh methods and perspectives on the Bible continually reshape how we view it and how it nourishes us. New developments and understandings about ourselves and our societies constantly reconstruct our grasp of who we are and what we are to do. Of course we can take only so much "rethinking" at any one time, and there are moments of consolidation between the breakthroughs and new syntheses. The point is that our challenge is not to find ways to fuse two horizons that are solidly fixed, but to relate horizons that themselves undergo change. If this seems frightening, the very possibility of fusing the horizons often depends on our capacity to re-vision one or both of them.

The Ethical Horizons Must Be Fused with Caution

What do we mean when we say that our ethics are biblically informed ethics, that we approach eco-justice issues, for example, in a manner that conforms to the Bible? When we think of ethics we are likely to emphasize ethical decisions, on the one hand, and ethical principles or ideals, on the other. Recent studies of the Bible in Christian ethics[4] have emphasized that ethics are historically contextual and touch on matters of feeling and desire. Perhaps more crucial than the Bible's direct contribution to our ethical decision-making is its pervasive function in our moral formation, inclining us toward values and feelings that shape a moral matrix or climate. Probably the stories, characters, and images of the Bible have as much to do with this moral formation as the specific ethical teaching of the Bible. This kind of overall moral formation by the Bible allows us to move "biblically," as it were, in areas that the Bible does not touch, and also allows us to reach conclusions which are other than those reached by biblical writers on specific matters.

The Social Placement of the Horizons
Is Critical for Re-visioning

If there is any one way in which our horizon is most unlike the biblical horizon, it has to do with premises about the social character of human existence. The Bible posits a social matrix for human meanings and actions that is no longer to be taken for granted and indeed is often scarcely recognized. Along with the undoubted gains of heightened personalism in modern life has gone an atomistic individualism which, taken at the extreme, makes the Bible practically unintelligible. In practice, this means that we can fuse the horizons meaningfully only if we pay special attention to how biblical texts are socially placed and how our thoughts, concerns, and projects are socially placed. The urge toward generality and universalism in our reading of the Bible and ourselves must be tempered by the steadily asked questions: Who is speaking *in these texts*? For whom and about whom are *we* speaking? This is to recognize that the communication of God is always and everywhere a communication to people in social contexts.

The Social Placement of Our Horizon
Must Be Concretized

It is all well and good to acknowledge in principle that we are social beings. It is a far more demanding task, both humbling and empowering, to specify as precisely as we can what our social placement actually is. Since the interests of the political economy and the drift of culture work strongly against this kind of social knowledge, we can come by it only through hard work. Because the knowledge is *social* knowledge, we can only attain it by working together; it is not a project for rugged individualism, although it may

take some of the reputed courage of the individualist to
face up to the realities discovered.

In terms of biblical interpretation, a way to begin the
inquiry about our social horizon is to ask, What are the
factors at play in the way that I and my community are
disposed to understand the Bible on eco-justice concerns?
A small working group at New York Theological Seminary
has begun to try to formulate these factors. So far we have
identified the following:

1. What is my/our church history and tradition?
2. What is my/our formal or informal theology?
3. Who is the interpreting authority for me/us?
4. What is my/our ethnic identity?
5. What is my/our educational level and specialization?
6. What is my/our social class?
7. What is my/our gender identity?
8. What is my/our explicit political position?
9. What is my/our political "valence," i.e., what political moods or directions do I/we tend to support or favor even when not active or vocal?
10. What customary use of the Bible do I/we practice?
11. What translation or study Bible do I/we use?
12. What forms of liturgy and spirituality do I/we practice?

Some of these questions are not easy to answer. We also
recognize early on that we may be individually formed by
different communities from different periods of our lives
and that the communities to which we now belong may
have various subgroups and tendencies within them. The
inventory of questions is simply a prompter to help us look
at areas we might otherwise pass over. The most interesting and important question by far is how the mix of factors
works in given persons and communities. The end result of
this inquiry into the political and social hermeneutics that
inform us should be to increase our self-awareness and
help us to decide which elements we want to keep or

discard, which we want to alter, and how we might wish to reassess the priorities of the elements now that we are more conscious of their operation every time we go to biblical texts or form an impression about "what the Bible says."

This reflection on fusing biblical and contemporary horizons would not be complete without attention to the social placement of the biblical horizon.[5]

II. The Social Placement of the Early Biblical Horizon

Biblical religion and society extend over more than a thousand years of time. This means that there are in fact many biblical horizons. I want to accent the formative period in premonarchic Israel, in part because I know it best and in part because that formative period sets a stage and an agenda that persist throughout biblical times, even though conditions of life change greatly. For example, one of the texts suggested as the basis for an eco-justice sermon is Ezekiel 34:1–16. Although this text speaks of "the shepherds of Israel" in exilic times, I would contend that its sociopolitical premises about communal leadership were shaped in the premonarchic origins of Israel.

Simply put, my reconstruction of earliest Israel yields the profile of an agrarian social revolution whose ideology or moving spirit and rationale was the religion of Yahweh.[6] The chief features of this movement in its history and organizational structure are as follows:

1. In origin, the first Israelites were largely members of *lower or marginal classes* within powerful Canaanite city-states. The agricultural and pastoral products of these common people accrued to bureaucrats, merchants, and large landowners, all of whom lived as parasites on the people at large. Thus, the Israelites were not pastoral nomadic outsiders or invaders who took over what belonged to others, but they were depressed "insiders," claiming the wealth that they produced by their own labor.

2. These Israelites were a people of *mixed origins* in their ethnic and cultural identities. Socioeconomically, they were

mostly peasants, but they also included herders, artisans, mercenary troops, and priests.

3. Israel emerged into history as a *revolutionary social movement*, taking the means of production in land solely into its own hands, breaking the iron grip of the state and its client classes over the life and goods of the general populace. The nearest analogies to the manner of waging this struggle appear to be the successful peasant wars of the twentieth century, such as those that have taken place in Mexico, Russia, China, Vietnam, Algeria, and Cuba.[7]

4. Israel arose as a coalition of peoples whose movement for liberation was made possible by large-scale *social cooperation and combination* among diverse previously unempowered groups.

5. Israel constituted a broadly *tribal people* who organized self-rule, self-defense, mutual aid networks, and cultural self-expression in cooperative forms that delegated necessary leadership, all the while struggling to restrict the leadership so that it did not usurp the means of production and undermine the equality of the people.

6. The people of Israel were of *approximate equality*, living in large extended families and protective associations (often called clans), a people with basically the same rights to life resources, which for them meant land and its produce and raw materials. They paid no taxes in kind, nor did they render military service or draft labor to kings or ruling classes. In Marxist terms, they benefited directly and totally from the use value of the products of their labor.

7. In order to break free from city-states and overlords and to form a viable community of their own, these first Israelites had to conduct *a people's war* for freedom and to forge *a people's culture* expressive of their self-confidence, self-determination, and shared values of at-homeness in their world.

8. The sharpest form of cultural self-expression among the Israelites was *a people's religion*. This religion, often called Yahwism after the name of the deity (Yahweh),

affirmed the unity of the people and their commitment to prevail in history as a society of mutually supportive equals. Their faith in Yahweh, the delivering and blessing God, affirmed their belief that they were supported by the highest existing power—a power immediately experienced in the common life of the people.

This formative period of biblical religion and society set a standard and a tone for all later phases of Israel's life. Even when Israel experienced a counterrevolution under its own monarchy and eventually fell into colonial subservience to great powers, it was remembered and expected that Israel should be an independent self-determining society of equals under one God. That production of the means of subsistence and reproduction of the biological and social bases of human life should go together in a harmonious whole presupposed eco-justice as the foundation of life mandated by God.

III. Covenant Faith Embraces Nature and Culture

Of the many implications and ramifications of this way of viewing the beginnings of Israel, I want to single out one that has very large consequences for how we think about the relation of religion to the rest of life and especially to the natural and social environments.

For some decades biblical theology cultivated the notion of biblical religion as history opposed to nature, and faith opposed to culture.[8] Thus, Canaanite religion and society stood for a chain of associated ideas that went something like this: polytheism = femininity = weakness = cultural compromise = natural cycles = "bad." Israelite religion and society stood for another chain of associated ideas in this fashion: monotheism = masculinity = virility = historical action = covenant faith = "good."

This pair of polarized paradigms is faulty history and theology. Yahweh's "masculinity" affirms continuity and culture: the notions of Yahweh as "father" and as "deliverer/protector" are sociopolitical and natural/familial notions, applicable to divine involvement in history and nature. Yahweh's "femininity" is fully located within a covenantal context and stresses aspects of the blessing/fecundity paradigm that persistently accompanies the deliverance/virility paradigm.

The God of social-revolutionary Israel was simply *not* discontinuous with natural processes and the social order as such. Yahweh was correspondent to and continuous with the natural processes on which the Israelite cultivators depended, and Yahweh was likewise correspondent to and continuous with the social thrust of retribalization. Israel made the claim in its own retribalizing of social activity and in its religious proclamation that nature and history were both malleable and good: they belonged to Yahweh and the people of Yahweh. Sexuality, as an aspect of the natural and social whole, was likewise good.

Consequently, I believe that we must say that covenantal thinking in early Israel was not faith *against* culture but faith *sustaining one form of culture against another form of culture:* Israelite *participatory* culture against Canaanite *hierarchic* culture. There never was a moment in Israelite Yahwism when its theological assertions were only or primarily against culture, whether the Canaanite culture or culture in general. From the start Israelite Yahwism affirmed and sustained an alternative way of appropriating natural and social goods through an alternative culture. It is absolutely essential to grasp the faith/culture problematic, not as an abstract division between faith and culture, but as a sharp juxtaposition of one faith/culture structure against another faith/culture structure in a contest over the appropriation of the same natural and social goods.

The split between religion and society, between faith and culture, that has come to dominate Western thought has been rudely and erroneously retrojected into the origins of Western religion. There is of course no self-evident way to bring these severed terms back into vital connection, least of all by some simpleminded attempt to restore "biblical religion." Nonetheless, our own contribution toward a religiously informed eco-justice will be impossible without a re-visioning of our biblical foundations.[9]

Again and again we settle for a one-sidedly "religious" account of Israel, as though the covenant were simply a spiritual connection. In fact, the covenant basis of Israel was a simultaneously religious and sociopolitical reality with effects in nature and history. It reflected and posited a society of equals possessing the earth and living together in mutual respect and just order.

IV. The Bible as an Eco-Justice Resource

The history of appeals to the Bible to justify opposing positions on all kinds of issues is at first discouraging but ultimately instructive if we keep in mind the social placement of the horizons from which biblical interpreters operate. This is why the self-examination of our own placement in society is so important. Willard M. Swartley, in a careful analysis of four case issues in biblical interpretation, shows how actual biblical interpreters came to differing views about slavery, Sabbath observance, war, and women.[10] The fact that slavery and Sabbath observance are now less debated issues than war and women allows us to look both at disputes that have "cooled down" and at disputes that have "heated up."

At the close of his study, Swartley reviews some of the predominant views about the way the Bible relates to social issues, and whether and how the biblical and contemporary horizons can be fused. His spectrum of positions is not unlike the one laid out by H. Richard Niebuhr in his classic work *Christ and Culture.* I list Swartley's version of six alternative views,[11] together with the advocates he identifies, although it would be easy to add many other names since the views are recognizable as widely shared options:

1. The New Testament has no useful social ethic for us because it is so thoroughly eschatological (Jack T. Sanders).

2. The Bible has clear social-ethical teachings, but neither Jesus nor Paul changed social structures (Rudolf Schnackenburg).

3. Biblical teaching speaks to social-ethical issues and calls the church to prophetic witness (John H. Yoder).

4. The Bible influences social ethics through the moral formation and identity of God's people in numerous ways (Bruce Birch and Larry Rasmussen).

5. The Bible stresses God's action and the church as the locus of the new order (four German biblical scholars working as a study group: Jürgen Kegler, Peter Lampe, Paul Hoffmann, and Ulrich Luz).

6. Analysis of the social situation is a prerequisite for understanding the Bible's social ethic (Juan Luis Segundo).

It seems to me that there is some element of truth to be taken into account in each of these positions. In my judgment, no one of them is complete in itself, and the way to a better biblical grounding for eco-justice will not be through patching together theories from various sources. We have to reenvision and bring a critique to both horizons in a most thorough and determined way. And we must somehow do that with more collegiality among scholars, ministers, and laity, as also among biblical scholars, ethicists, and theologians. I concur in the emphasis of Segundo on getting a better grasp of social situation, both the Bible's and our own, because this is an indispensable feature of our faith as well as of our eco-justice quandaries. Over the course of Christian history, social situation has been the most neglected of all the dimensions of the hermeneutical task.

V. Obstacles to an Adequate Fusion of Horizons

It may seem downbeat and low-spirited to end my presentation with a look at the obstacles to be overcome. I do so because we must face and size up the enormity of the task before us by fully grasping the structural and ideological realities that work so steadily against a clearheaded fusion of horizons. The obstacles that seem most serious to me are as follows:

1. We lack concrete information about and awareness of situations, systems, and processes of eco-justice and eco-injustice.

2. We are taught by church and society to treat poverty, waste, and oppression as matters to be corrected by goodwill and individual effort.

3. We avoid oppression and inequity by withdrawing into private pursuits and personal religion.

4. We confuse reconciliation and grace with tolerance and accommodation toward injustice.

5. We deny and suppress the reality of conflict and system-cultivated violence through false appeals to unity, love, and nonviolence that do not attack the roots of eco-injustice.

6. We substitute discussions, ideals, doctrines, good intentions, churchgoing, even Bible-reading, for critical thinking and justice-doing.

7. We derive benefits from injustice, direct or indirect, that we do not want to jeopardize, and sometimes these benefits accrue to the church.

8. We do not have the personal courage to sustain critical thinking and acting.

In reciting this list I realize the danger of ending with yet another "white liberal guilt trip." That would of course only confirm us in our impotence and lack of imagination. I prefer rather that we think of these obstacles as opportunities. Sometimes the best way to attack a problem is to confront the points where we keep excusing ourselves from the hard work necessary to formulate the problem in an approachable manner.[12]

One thing that my understanding of the comprehensive socioreligious origins of Israel suggests to me is that we have a mandate to tell the church about the truth of early

Israel. It is after all the church's glory to preach and teach its Scripture. It is the agenda of the church to keep abreast of the best understanding of its Bible available. When the social holism of early Israel is preached and taught, the biblical horizon raises questions and issues challenges to our privatism and withdrawal. Our Bible tells us that in some fundamental ways we are out of touch with its power and genius. Evoking a holistic biblical horizon may be a key step in reshaping our own horizon to the point that eco-justice is not just a Christian obligation but a Christian joy. Recovery of the biblical social horizon together with the pain and terror of our own horizon might even convince us that struggle for eco-justice is the most authentic and urgent way to be Christian in this moment of history.

3

Preaching in the
Contemporary World

James A. Forbes

Like the apostle Paul, I need to confess that I once fought against what I now proclaim—in my case, concern for ecology. I feared that it was a new cause designed to obscure the unfinished business of racial and economic justice. Talk about the "greening of America" was designed, I thought, to push to the back burner a concern for the poor and oppressed minorities of our country and the rest of the world. Clearly I am not being pressed into duty as an official priest of the "E-J Movement," but rather because I am a minister of Jesus Christ, a preacher and a teacher of preachers. It seems high time to take a closer look at the relationship between my discipline of preaching and the growing concern and call for eco-justice.

From my crash course and minibriefing on eco-justice, I've come to identify the following concerns as central:

1. Creation must be viewed holistically as comprising its human and nonhuman aspects as integral parts of each other.

2. In any biblical understanding, "the Fall" will not be viewed simply as bringing so-called "spiritual" consequences but also as causing fragmentation, pollution, and alienation in the whole of the created order.

3. There must be a joyous and sober acceptance of our responsibility as stewards of the earth.

4. There must be a recognition of limits as we strive to

cultivate, enjoy, and conserve the resources of the earth. Nature must be understood as co-victim with the poor.

5. Christian maturity must include aspirations toward relational harmony based on a recognition of the interdependence of all forms of life. A unique style of life flows from this awareness and approach to human fulfillment.

6. The impulse to progress must be chastened by vigilance regarding the social and environmental impact of the varied means we employ to enjoy the human and natural gifts of God.

7. There must be a keen sense of mutual participation in building a new future which is sustainable in terms of adequate natural resources, firmly built on peace through economic and political justice.

8. Attempts to deal with national crises of health, production, and social dysfunction must be approached in the light of global awareness.

9. A loss of a sense of accountability and grateful participation with God will result in crisis after crisis in all areas of life.

If we understand and affirm such a perspective with its consciousness of the interconnection of all things, are we ready to set out on an eco-justice preaching mission? Perhaps not so soon. There is always the temptation to make a premature declaration of readiness—to purchase the bumper stickers and write an article for the newsletter or announce a sermon series on "Eco-Justice—The Heart of the Gospel." Before a preacher volunteers as a chief advocate of the movement, a deeper sense of self-awareness would seem to be required. Preachers would do well to "exegete" themselves to determine the level of commitment to the cause. A surface embrace of the slogans and symbols of the movement may be just enough to immunize the preacher and the congregation against a serious case of conviction on the issue. One or two sermons and seminars, while possibly helpful in a preliminary way, may be just enough to tempt the congregation to rest assured that we've covered that issue and we are now an official eco-justice parish.

Indications are that the values at the heart of eco-justice thinking may be in significant contrast and counterpoint to accustomed operative trends of thought in our culture today. The comprehensiveness and the interpenetration of interests and enterprises suggested in ecological sensitivity are in tension with the more personal and provincial considerations which have a stronger claim on our limited time and attention. Gentle broadening of perspective will not be enough. What is called for is a radical revisioning of the nature of the world and our place and responsibility in it.

Preparation for eco-justice preaching involves not only heightened personal awareness for the preacher but also serious cultural analysis. Even though preaching is done in the context of a faith-claiming community, the claims of the culture or social milieu are stronger than we sometimes assume. The times and currents in which we live are manifested as strong living forces, occupying the decision-making centers deep within us. With such forces, faith claims must contend constantly.

In some circles there is an emerging awareness of reduced resources. There is declining confidence in the prospect for continuous progress in the years ahead. In the wake of scientific and technological advance, coupled with the increased efficiency in social and bureaucratic control, there is declining belief in the relevance of the transcendent for the dimensions of life which concern most people in our culture. Secularization is not only affecting faith commitment but also causing the erosion of loyalty in response to political authority. There is a growing sense of crisis, with a plethora of reasons for our problems and as many solutions for them. Yet there is a growing despair about the inadequacy of all the proposed plans of deliverance. In response to such tensions one is able to discern narcissistic preoccupation, a narrowing of the range of vision as one

seeks to cope with the threatening imponderables, a reduced tolerance for complexity and insecurity, and perhaps a willingness to yield up freedom in exchange for
strong-armed political promises to protect against a multiplicity of alien forces.

It is into this cultural context that the broadening and
transformative vision of eco-justice must be preached. We
have our work cut out for us. Such preaching will of
necessity be countercultural in a profound sense. It will
require forms of austerity not usually embraced by those
who feel insecure. It will challenge "haves" to give serious
consideration to altering their consumption. New patterns
of resource distribution will need to be developed. The
eco-justice agenda will require moral, mental, spiritual,
and social transformation of major proportions.

Were there no advance cadre of persons already moving
in the direction of ecological sensitivity, our task would
seem well nigh impossible. It is gratifying to report that the
eco-justice movement is growing and gathering support
from a broadening cross-section of clergy and laity. Peri-
odicals, workshops, and modest offices are appearing here
and there, which suggests that seeds are growing. Such
beginnings will require the strengthening impact of our
pulpits to call the church to faithfulness. Let us turn now to
consider what kind of preaching will provide that support
and inspire fresh vision as we respond to the call for
wholeness and relatedness.

I. Concept

The kind of preaching required to bring our nation to
ecological consciousness and commitment is preaching
designed for radical transformation. In using the word
"radical" I do not mean to suggest something reckless,
obstructionist, or destructive in spirit, but rather an intention to touch the roots in persons where values give rise to
motivation and action. In calling for transformation the
judgment is made that our basic orientation to life is

contrary to the divine intent. A fundamental shift in perspective and approach to life must be effected. Preaching which is not this ambitious will not fill the bill. Nor would I wish to give the impression that such preaching is always out for spectacular evidence of change immediately following each homily. A mature understanding of radical change respects minute shifts as contributive to major reorientation.

But is not the above a description of the goal of preaching at its best whether the issue is eco-justice, regeneration, or freedom from fear? An understanding of preaching which does not include "root canal" surgery is deficient. If the preacher is always content simply to give a gentle push in the direction of prevailing trends, the scope of the gospel's agenda has been greatly reduced from its original call to repentance and restoration.

Preaching is an event in which the living Word of God is proclaimed in the power of the Holy Spirit. It is that process in which the preacher serves to activate the dialogue between God and the people as they gather as a community of faith. It is the context in which the transforming power of the truth of the gospel is addressed to the concrete realities of daily existence as well as the ultimate issues of eternal significance. Preaching is a dynamic divine/human interaction in which the people of God are nourished for the journey of life and are empowered to serve and to celebrate the present and coming kingdom of God.

Preaching thus understood is not primarily rationalistic or characterized by stylistic appeal. It moves people. It gathers people, forms them into community, informs them, transforms them, refreshes, empowers, and releases them. If one intends to effect life-style changes through preaching, strong verbs will be called into the process. Much of the preaching of our time lacks some of the more dynamic dimensions. Subtle suggestion when used intentionally will function toward profound alteration of outlook. Where gentle socialization seems in order it will have deprogramming intent. Howard Thurman used to speak of the word touching "the nerve center of consent." This is important because the internal operative concept one holds sets limits on the pattern of proclamation. Most preachers do that which their reigning conceptualizations dictate. To help toward a more powerful pulpit will require a change in concept.

II. The Spirit of Eco-Justice Preaching

A new spirit will be demanded as one goes about the task of eco-justice preaching. In the first place, there will be respect for and knowledge of what is going on in the world of our hearers. To call people out of the ways of the world places the responsibility upon the preacher to know what the world is like, what its trends are, how it commands allegiance from its subjects, how tenaciously it holds them hostage, how deeply etched are its mandates. Otherwise the habits of preconscious formation will ridicule the puny assault upon their dominating influence. For example, the advertising industry will write boldly about ways to prevent defection from the cult of conspicuous consumption. How naive are the sermons which scold or seek to stir up guilt when the addiction to destructive behavior is stronger than the impulse to freedom. To cast out the demons of rapacious exploitation of the earth's resources requires the eco-justice exorcist to know what she or he is up against.

We must not only know the world of our hearers, but must be prepared to begin where they are and, even more important, to enlist their participation in the process of conceiving new desirabilities and possibilities. Gung-ho advocates of change often become so disgusted with the dreadfully unenlightened belief system of the people that they practically invalidate the places where people are as acceptable starting points toward enlightenment. But condemnation of where people are unduly delays the process of building new patterns of response. As Christians we are impressed with the qualities Jesus was able to call forth from his disciples. What we tend to overlook is the extraordinary optimism and patience of Jesus in accepting the motley recruits just as they were. He even freed them to express what was in them so that they could see and hear more clearly their ignorance or see what spirit they were of. Preachers who show patience and respect for persons regardless of the inadequacy of their present understanding are more likely to get the opportunity to lead them toward more light.

Our discussion has given a prominent place to the work of the Spirit. The eco-justice agenda is broader than our ordinary human projects. It touches issues from the survival instinct of individuals to the second law of thermodynamics. Reliance upon the Spirit in these matters springs from our recognition that uncommon vision and vitality are essential to the tasks we undertake. For all our psychological insight we have not solved the problem of how to promote freedom so that people will rise above inordinate self-regard and promote the well-being of their neighbors. And even if such a miracle discovery were made, would we be able to offer the blueprint for cosmic harmony among all things? For all our positive virtues we need a coordinator of more comprehensive scope and power. This is why the Spirit is so central to these considerations.

III. Content of the Preaching

If one feels called to the vocation being described here, there may be an eagerness to start a collection of choice biblical texts for eco-justice preaching. Obviously such a list would be of some value. However, the task involves more than finding proof texts. In fact, one cannot be content with traditional theological resources alone. One is called upon to deal with a multiplicity of disciplines and knowledge areas. Politics, agriculture, business, law, geography, economics, and psychology are intertwined with the issues under consideration. The scope of eco-justice concerns demands the broadening of the horizons of interests and general understandings. For an example, serious concern for energy development and conservation will lead to discussion of technology, biology, physics, sociology, politics, communication, and transportation. It is not enough to be a student of the Book; there are many books which need to be read if one is to achieve competence in these matters.

In addition to traditional religious issues an eco-justice preacher will have an understanding of the prevailing worldview represented in the cultural context where he or she does ministry. There will also be continuous updating of information regarding the main currents on the world scene. The scope of these problems will demand a recognition that the world is our parish, at least in a sense. Preachers will no longer avoid systems analysis or social, political, and economic critique. No one will be able to convince them that such matters are none of the preacher's business. Everything which affects the common space we inhabit becomes worthy of reflection and comment. The preacher will develop a keen sense of the interrelatedness of all things, centered and grounded in the God of faith.

All the general subjects we have described above do not substitute for solid biblical/theological understanding. Indeed, there will be a fresh impetus toward a deepening and broadening competency in doctrinal matters. Eco-justice preachers will find themselves reviewing the doctrines of creation and salvation, biblical principles of stewardship, theologies of nature and natural theology, Christian anthropology and eschatology, foundational principles of personal and international ethics, concern for spiritual formation of persons in congregations for qualitative witness in the world, and the Spirit's call from war and oppression to peace and power for all.

Does this outline of the task place eco-justice preaching beyond the present level of preparedness of most pastors and preachers? If one must demonstrate mastery before beginning the task, there will be very few voices crying in the wilderness. But if faith-and-commitment-seeking-understanding is an appropriate starting place, no one need delay. The magnitude of the task should cause sober acknowledgment of inadequacy. But this is not new. The objectives of preaching have always been more demanding than our human resources alone could meet. Preachers who understand this will be able to act without pretensions to omniscience or omnipotence. We are unable to do all that needs to be done, but we can do what we can in confidence that the Spirit will incorporate our faithful efforts into the *magnum opus* of the Sovereign One.

One of my favorite stories is a Sufi tale filled with ecological wisdom. It is called the Tale of the Sands. It is about a little stream that wanted to cross the desert. Each time it tried it would be swallowed up in the hot desert sand. But one day a voice was heard reassuring the stream that it could cross the desert. When the stream inquired of the voice, this is what it was told.

"By hurtling in your own accustomed way you cannot get across. You will either disappear or become a marsh. You must allow the wind to carry you over, to your destination."

The stream could cross the desert by allowing itself to be absorbed in the wind. But the stream objected to this idea, since it had never been absorbed before. The stream wanted to maintain its individuality. If that were lost, how could the stream be itself?

"The wind," said the sand, "takes up water, carries it over the desert, and then lets it fall again. Falling as rain, the water again becomes a river."

The voice reminded the stream that its essential part is always being carried away to form a stream again, and this essential part is always elusive. So the stream raised its vapor into the welcoming arms of the wind, which bore it along gently and easily, letting it fall in the mountains miles away.

In this way, the stream learned its true identity from the sands which extend from the riverside all the way to the mountain. Thus it is said that the way traversed by the Stream of Life is written in the Sands.[1]

In relatedness, respect, and reliance upon the help of the other is the prospect of fulfillment. Wind, sand, and the mountains play their part in sustaining the flow of the streams of life. There is also the voice which speaks what is written in the sand.

In Isaiah 35 we hear about a stream which flows again:

> For waters shall break forth in the wilderness,
>   and streams in the desert;
> The burning sand shall become a pool,
>   and the thirsty ground springs of water.
>   (Isaiah 35:6b–7a)

And in Revelation 22 we read:

> Then he showed me the river of the water of life, bright as crystal, flowing from the throne of God and of the Lamb through the middle of the street of the city; also, on either side of the river, the tree of life with its twelve kinds of fruit, yielding its fruit each month; and the leaves of the tree were for the healing of the nations. (Revelation 22:1–2)

Thus is the drama of restoration echoed throughout the Bible.

4

Proclaiming Liberation for the Earth's Sake

E. David Willis

Any theology of proclamation today must be done under the nuclear cloud which threatens not just humanity but also humanity's co-creature, the earth. We may bemoan the stereotype of preaching delivered by the so-called preacher in the TV film *The Day After,* but our task is to consider the nature of the preaching which must occur as *a part of* what the Christian community can do to help turn the tide which does indeed seem to be relentlessly moving us all toward nuclear war. Preaching is, humanly speaking, frail in the face of the complexity and magnitude of the contemporary crisis. That, I assume, can be taken for granted. The question before us is, What is the nature of preaching that is a means of equipping the Christian community for its simultaneous involvement in a wide range of active witnessing in different structures of society? While the focus is on preaching, preaching itself cannot be properly understood apart from other ways proclamation occurs.[1] Thus I shall explore the significance of the sacraments in proclaiming liberation today.

I. The Ecclesial Reality in Praxis

Of the numerous analyses of the ethics of peacemaking, I find that of Stanley Hauerwas particularly helpful in pinpointing at least the problem which must be addressed to gain a coherent approach in this crisis. He argues that the challenge of nuclear weapons involves issues that require a theological response, but one which our culture at large lacks the resources to provide. Moreover, those already attempting to provide theological resources are hampered in their efforts because of a confusion about eschatologies.

> The peace sought by many is too often equivalent to order while lacking a sufficient sense of what a just peace entails. . . . A peace based on insufficient eschatology cannot but be an abstract ideal that lacks concrete embodiment in the lives and habits of an actual community. Moreover, without such a community our strategies for nuclear disarmament as well as the moral resources on which they draw cannot help but offer short-term solutions and false consolation.[2]

While I do not entirely agree with his treatment of eschatology, Hauerwas is quite right that effective peacemaking requires not just an ideal but concrete embodiment in the lives and habits of an actual community. I want to lift up the liberated and liberating nature of such a community as essential to understanding the connection between peace and justice and practicing their connection.

The same point about the necessity of communal embodiment is made in what remains a classic presentation of liberation theology, namely Gustavo Gutiérrez' *A Theology of Liberation*. In the methodological section, Gutiérrez is quite explicit about a matter that is strangely overlooked or minimized in many subsequent theologies of liberation: This theology is critical reflection not just on praxis in general but on *ecclesial* praxis.

> Our purpose is not to elaborate an ideology to justify postures already taken, nor to undertake a feverish search for security in the face of the radical challenges which confront the faith, nor to fashion a theology from which political action is "deduced." It is rather to let ourselves be judged by the Word of the Lord, to think through the faith, to strengthen our love, and to give reason for our hope from within a commitment which seeks to become more radical, total, and efficacious.[3]

Such theology as critical reflection on ecclesial praxis does not replace theology in its other aspects (as wisdom and rational knowledge), but presupposes them and helps redefine them. In each of its forms, however, and surely in the form of critical reflection on ecclesial praxis, theology is a communal activity—precisely of that community which is constituted, corrected, and empowered by the Word which confronts men and women in their own concrete situations. That Word is addressed to church and to world, and so implies a criticism of both. In its coming to the church, the Word calls, liberates, and empowers men and women who are inevitably engaged in the critical sociocultural and economic issues of their lives.

> Theological reflection would then necessarily be a criticism of society and the Church insofar as they are called and addressed by the Word of God; it would be a critical theory, worked out in the light of the Word accepted in faith and inspired by a practical purpose—and therefore indissolubly linked to historical praxis. By preaching the Gospel message, by its sacraments, and by the charity of its members, the Church proclaims and shelters the gift of the Kingdom of God in the heart of human history. The Christian community professes a faith which works through charity.[4]

The ecclesial context of liberating preaching is easily either overlooked or else presupposed in a view of preaching which suggests a bypassing of its centrality. It is easy to think of preaching as communicating certain ideas to a congregation and thereby instructing them and moving them as individuals to specific tasks. That, of course, is involved. But when preaching is seen as Word-event which is constitutive of ecclesial reality, a slightly different model emerges—one which takes seriously ethical action as living-out, as embodying in the whole of life, the communal reality which is brought into being, continually corrected, and empowered as a liberated and liberating factor in the world. This fleshing-out, as it were, of the gospel in a community of faith-active-in-love obviously involves individual commitment and action. But there is a world of difference between, on the one hand, inspired and instructed individuals acting ethically, and, on the other, a community taking worldly shape as an effective sign of the reality that God wills and works—even outside the church—to bring about for the whole of creation.

When there is a loss of the sense of the church, the nature of preaching has been significantly misconstrued and the force of ethical action significantly diluted and diffused. It is not that preaching does not get done and done well, or that ethical action does not occur; I am not arguing that. I am just calling attention to what I perceive as a serious gap in what may have been taken for granted in the past, one which can no longer be left unattended if we are to help provide the theological resources for coping with the present crisis.[5] When we bypass the ecclesial nature of praxis, we impoverish the range of symbols and of hope-engendering, future-shaping memory which give a community the identity out of which it can bring leverage to bear on the concrete ethical demands of the present. When the ecclesial reality is so taken for granted that it is virtually ignored, there is a dulling and a shrinking of the imagination. By imagination here I mean the process by which normative symbols and metaphors of the Christian community correct and transform the images people have of themselves, of others, and of the world. This process of imagination is one by which a community continually renews its identity, motivation, and significance. This bears directly on the nature of preaching, for preaching is one of the indispensable ways by which the community responds creatively to the normative symbols through which the Word is accommodated to our condition.

II. The Liberating Word Humanly Speaking

What I have said so far (and this goes at least for Gutiérrez' presuppositions) all hangs on what is meant by the Word. It makes all the difference in the world whether

preaching is *just* human communication or whether
preaching is *also and preeminently* a form of the Word of
God.[6] Ecclesial praxis is the activity of that community
which is gathered, built up, and sent by the Word of God
accommodating to our condition. Earlier I said we could
take it for granted that preaching is frail "humanly speaking" when compared with the enormity of the crisis facing
us. By that I meant something technical, namely, that
preaching is nothing less than *God's Word humanly speaking:*
God addressing to us the creating, delivering, sanctifying
Word through forgiven sinners used for that purpose. The
living God is the controlling agent in the Word-event which
is preaching. That event occurs ultimately by grace alone,
that is, by the favor and empowerment of the God whom
we know in Jesus Christ by the power of the Spirit.

The message is a rearticulation of what was proclaimed
by the one whom the apostles remembered and proclaimed
to be the Christ. Because the kingdom of God is at hand we
are called and enabled to repent and live in a new way in
the last times. That is to say, the message of Jesus (as
available to us in the proclamatory accounts of Jesus which
were shaped by the earliest community's experience of his
death and resurrection) is inseparable from the message
about Jesus. The radical character of ecclesial praxis depends on the radical character not only of Jesus' message
but also of who Jesus is as the Christ and what therefore his
saving work is.[7] Variously put, Jesus is "the Christ, the Son
of the living God," the eschatological figure "Son of Man,"
and "the coming one," "the anointed," in whom the proph-
ecy is fulfilled that the blind will see, the lame walk, the
lepers be cleansed, and the poor hear the good news that
the great day of the Lord and of their deliverance is at hand.

Even these claims are not sufficiently radical, for the
development of Christology in the New Testament includes the daring confession that this Jesus the Christ is the
creating, enlightening, life-giving Word in human form.
The proclamation in this claim is that Jesus the Christ has
significance for the cosmos, indeed, that the Word by

whom all things were made became a human being and dwelt among us, full of grace and truth. These Johannine themes are expanded until we actually have the claim in the later epistles that God's economy from before the foundation of the world was disclosed and effected by this Christ—indeed that eventually all things will find their recapitulation, their gathering together under one head, in him. This development is foundational to the necessarily radical character of the liberating message: that in Jesus the Christ God has actually taken on the condition not just of alienated, oppressed and oppressing humanity, but of alienated creation in the form of a finite human being.[8] This is the extent of the solidarity which God's loving justice and just loving establishes with those caught in the web of alienation: God takes the place of, stands in the stead of, lives through, the condition of creatures.

III. The Worldliness of Confessional Hermeneutics

The language we have been using arises from within a definite hermeneutical context provided by two social environments: our participation in the confessing tradition of the one holy, catholic, and apostolic church; and our participation in the liberating presence and activity of the Triune God in the world. Since neither of these claims is obvious, a word is in order about each as a given of the hermeneutical task which is involved in preaching.

There is no such thing as uninterpreted Word of God. Each form of the Word (incarnate as revelation in Jesus the Christ; written testimony to that revelation as Old and New Testament; proclamation out of the Scriptures to Jesus the Christ) is available to us only through a series of hermeneutical actions. An interpretive process is already going on in the remembrance and proclamation[9] of who Jesus is and what he does as the Christ, so that the Scriptures themselves result from a range of hermeneutical activities. The interpretation of Scripture in subsequent cultures and generations is inevitably done with changing perspectives if the gospel is to be the gospel to men and women outside the chronology and geography of the ancient Mediterranean basin. The ecumenical creeds serve as subordinate standards of the church's faith insofar as they are the result of establishing the boundaries within which God's activity and presence in Jesus the Christ for the whole inhabited earth can be confessed, taught, and used doxologically. The need to reconfess the catholic faith continues in the face of those dangers from within and without the church which would cut short or diminish the inclusiveness of the proclamation of the gospel in subsequent cultures and generations. The *content* of the ecumenical creeds and subsequent confessions is important for guiding later instances of the church's confessing life. Their content is important in the measure that they are themselves reinterpreted in the light of the historical circumstances which evoked and shaped them and in the light of the subsequent exigencies demanding the church's witness. But almost equally as important as the specific content of the confessions is the trajectory and momentum, the sense of hope and future-shaping memory, which the history of this confessing tradition provides.[10]

A good example of how this confessing tradition functions is the Barmen Declaration, whose fiftieth anniversary we celebrated in 1984. It was drawn up by people who saw the church confronted by the exercise of a lordship over men and women alien to the Lordship of Christ. Those making that confession were emphatic in their claim to be speaking as members of the one holy, catholic, and apostolic church—indeed as those who bring forward and apply in their time not only the claims of the ecumenical creeds but also those of the confessions of the Reformation. And they spoke as persons in a definite time and place, as the Confessional Synod of the German Evangelical Church. The six famous "evangelical truths," of the Declaration, with the accompanying rejections of false doctrines, expound on the unifying theme of the meaning of Christ's ruling for the church and for the whole of life.

Jesus Christ, as he is attested for us in Holy Scripture, is the one
Word of God which we have to hear and which we have to trust
and obey in life and death. We reject the false doctrine, as
though the Church could and would have to acknowledge as a
source of its proclamation, apart from and besides this one
Word of God, still other events and powers, figures and truths,
as God's revelation. . . .

As Jesus Christ is God's assurance of the forgiveness of all
our sins, so in the same way and with the same seriousness he
is also God's mighty claim upon our whole life. Through him
befalls us a joyful deliverance from the godless fetters of this
world for a free, grateful service to his creatures. We reject the
false doctrine, as though there are areas of our life in which we
would not belong to Jesus Christ, but to other lords—areas
in which we would not need justification and sanctification
through him. (Declaration of Barmen, II, 1 and 2)[11]

The other social environment of this hermeneutical
context is one that is already put in Barmen's words,
"Through him befalls us a joyful deliverance *from* the
godless fetters of this world *for* a free, grateful service to
his creatures." (Emphasis added.) The particular godless
forms of bondage from which we are experiencing liberation were not all envisioned in Barmen; the movement of
God in that delivering action is, however, of one piece with
the stand being taken there. That is to say, liberation is not
just an occasional theme by which the good news is inter-
preted; it goes to the very heart of the message itself and to
the very heart of the delivering God. Deliverance is *from*
numerous forms of bondage experienced not just as cap-
tivity, as being bound, but as being oppressed, exploited by
what we can only point to as "godless." This deliverance is
at the very same time freedom *for* new forms and patterns
of service to other of God's creatures. The ecclesial reality
which participates in God's liberating-from/liberating-for
activity in the world engages in *a fresh hermeneutical enterprise which is itself part of that process of liberation.* A different
perspective is brought to bear on the tradition so that the
retraditioning of a people's hope-shaping and future-

shaping memory occurs to give men and women new historical consciousnesses and new history-altering activity.[12] This process is not, as it were, accidental to the church's or the gospel's substance; this process is part of the essential process by which the gospel once given continues to be God's Word for men and women in each new economic, political, cultural, sexual, racial, and aesthetic context. Indeed it is part of the essential process by which the church moves forward to the *fullness* of its unity, catholicity, holiness, and apostolicity, which is—technically—a future and eschatological reality.

IV. Christian Freedom and Human Liberation

Preaching, which is the liberating Word of God humanly speaking, includes an exposure of the godless fetters and a call to repentance. It is a deliverance of the "woe be unto you, for you have. . . ." Part of the process of conscientization is to engage men and women in that radical perspectival shift by which we come to see our enmeshment in the nexus of bondage and oppression. It is the Word of the Lord and not just a particular political preference which judges the systemic *misuse* of power that keeps people not "in their place" but exactly in the place which God does *not* intend for them. The liberating Word of God humanly speaking is literally "up-setting": the poor and those with none to plead their cause are exalted and their case is "taken up"[13] by the Word who takes on their condition, and the exalted are brought low and the mighty are "scattered in the vain imagination of their hearts." This is the Word addressed to us, for there is no possibility left us to escape this judgment by externalizing the evil onto others. It exposes the way in which love of God has become the self-love of our own egocentric predicament,[14] until we are so "curved in on" ourselves that we treat other people and the earth selfishly for our own self-interests and gluttony. This extends to the concupiscence which keeps others in the place God does *not* intend for them: in fetters

of racism, sexism, ageism, economic and political exploitation—and in the corruption, the pollution of the earth,
which nourishes us to our health or to our destruction.
This convicting Word brings us to startling awareness, to
awakening from a deep enchantment, until we cry with the
utmost urgency, "What must we do to be saved?"

This liberating Word of God humanly speaking is, above
all, the assurance of forgiveness and the power to live new
lives. The "No" of the "Woe unto you" is included in the
sovereign "Yes" of God's merciful judgment. It would be a
disastrous error to suggest that the judgment of God
belongs to the "No" and the mercy of God belongs only to
the "Yes." For God's judgment of us is mercifully just and
justly merciful. It is, after all, and beginning all, the
judgment which God has already rendered in the cross and
resurrection of Jesus the Christ. What if, at this decisive
point, we were to slip away from the theology of the cross[15]
and back into a subtle theology of glory by which we
defined both peace and justice abstractly or speculatively
and turned to the central saving action of God only for
illustration of what we have found better elsewhere? To do
so would be to relinquish the only real power which the
ecclesial reality actually has, that of proclaiming the message which is exclusively God's Word to and about the
human condition in the light of Christ's presence and
activity on humanity's behalf. The "No" itself is spoken in
love—even, and sometimes especially, in an angry love.
The aim of the "No" is to call God's people back to their
senses, as it were, to quicken consciences which have
become dulled and cold by habits, customs, structures,
ideologies of oppressive bondage. Such conscience-
quickening, such calling of God's people back from idolatry, is emphatically an action of God's mercy. It is the way
God does not leave us, as the prayerbook puts it, to "the
devices and desires of our own hearts."

The "Yes" is God's sovereign judgment; it is God overriding and crossing out our negation of self, of other
creatures, and of God. The good news is the forgiveness of

sin, the forgiveness of that to which God is unalterably opposed and that against which we must struggle all our life long. But the bottom line is that the gospel is the *forgiveness* of sin and the new power which that forgiveness brings to men and women so that they can walk in newness of life. If this central point is missed, what we preach is not the liberating Word of God but the petulance of those who have taken justice into their own hands and pronounce a false gospel which only spreads, deepens, and reinforces those patterns of oppressive and enslaving alienation which God's Word is out to overcome. Unless preaching ultimately is an assurance of forgiveness, all we do—not despite our best intentions but precisely because of our best intentions gone awry—is to produce paralyzing guilt and despair and so deprive men and women of the transforming power of hope.

Moltmann and others[16] have thoroughly described the function of hope in shaping one's understanding of and active participation in the shaping of history. Here I want only to underline something of the psychological dynamics of hope in the process of conscientization. That process does not merely expose the facts and dynamics of oppression to the oppressed and the oppressor. It brings about a powerful reimaging process by which men and women perceive themselves and their places in history differently. The oppressor and the oppressed alike are made conscious of their condition; that is already a reimaging act. Both are also given an image of themselves which transcends the now-realized oppressor/oppressed dependence; both see a vision of an alternative future in which the old image of self and of the other can be transformed. It is this reimaged future and this reimaged self as part of that future which draw men and women forward in transforming action. The assurance of forgiveness of sin is the most radical of messages precisely because it does not stop with exposing the old Adam but is an efficacious declaration— an accomplishing Word—that frees oppressor and oppressed from the bondage of their former selves and for the freedom of their future selves. Without the luring power of the future which comes with the forgiveness of sin, oppressor *and* oppressed inevitably cling to the security of the old Adam. Indeed, out of fear born of the ignorance of an alternative future, oppressed and oppressor will reinforce and stay with the oppressed/oppressor dependence. That is why the language of Barmen is so important in describing the "No" and the "Yes" which are present in deliverance from and deliverance for. "Through him befalls us a joyful deliverance from the godless fetters of this world for a free, grateful service to his creatures."

James Loder describes the character of convictional knowledge which is, I think, applicable to this place of hope in the process of conscientization. He describes five stages of "knowing as transforming event"[17] and shows how these stages are present in scientific knowing, aesthetic knowing, and therapeutic knowing. His analysis could extend to include economic-political knowing as transforming event. The five stages are: (1) confrontation with a crisis or problem, (2) conflict, (3) "scanning" (or weighing alternatives), (4) a constructive act of imagination, and (5) interpretation (which consolidates the new pattern as a plateau from which the process occurs again). This is applicable to our present task because, as I see it, preaching which is genuinely God's liberating Word humanly speaking moves men and women through these stages of knowing as transforming event. The crisis is exposed and conflict results; but to move beyond this stage we must be exposed to the range of alternatives, and to the reimaging which occurs with the assurance of the forgiveness of sin and the drawing power of the promised future.

V. The Liberating Word for the Earth

Thus far I have referred to the liberating Word's significance for service to other creatures without specifying the chief fellow creature about which the ecclesial praxis must have concern: the earth. That might seem an exaggeration, but only if we minimize the threat humanity poses to that fellow creature or if we uncritically adopt that portion of the tradition which defines anthropocentrically the earth's reason for being. Lynn T. White has long since called our attention to some of the negative effects on our natural environment of that portion of the creation saga which gives humanity dominion over the earth and other creatures on it. That saga does function positively to exalt humanity as of special concern and worth in God's eyes; but even there, humanity's worth and position is one of interdependence with the rest of creation. It is the *combination* of this positive esteem for humanity *with* a *utilitarian* view of the earth which proves to be so destructive. That results in the view that the earth is good to the extent that it provides resources for humanity.

We may even have competing views about the just distribution of the resources of the earth among people, without ever stepping outside the framework of this basically utilitarian treatment of the earth. Much of the prophetic appeal for more equitable distribution of resources and the prophetic protest against humanity's alienation from the fruit of labor were still based on an earlier presupposition that the earth's resources were "for all practical purposes" unlimited, and were so vast that human pollution could be absorbed and cleansed by the natural environment. There is a remarkable confidence in the perpetuation and healthiness of the earth and the heavens in the very imagery used to describe forms of human deliverance and wholeness: removal of sin leaves one whiter than snow; the magnitude of grace is like streams of living water; the people of God will be like a shoot out of a dry root, and so on. The fact that humanity can, and at an alarming rate does, pollute the snow, the streams, the plants, the heavens (which were earlier taken as a kind of steady backdrop for what really counted, namely, human destiny) involves us in a radical shift in our understanding of the inclusiveness of the liberating Word.

The liberating Word now has to address the question not

just of how humans must engage in forms of liberating themselves and others—but of how humanity in all its expressions must engage in liberating the earth from humanity's bondage and oppressive exploitation. Before I go further, though, a caveat must be sounded against those who would romantically and nostalgically dream of reversing the enormous strides already made in research into how the earth may be made to yield more food without depleting the soil. This is not the time, to put it mildly, for countering the progress made in determining and practicing ways by which humanity and other creatures may coexist. Environmental protection and saving species of wildlife from extinction require more, not less, technical expertise, political clout, funding, and international co-ordination. These forms of activity are in fact outworkings of the significance of the liberating Word for the earth's sake.

Nonetheless, such concern for environmental protection may still be just an extension of a fundamentally utilitarian approach to the earth. That model simply will not bear the weight of dealing with the magnitude of the crisis confronting humanity and the rest of the earth. For example, one runs into the argument (perhaps a self-protective defense against facing squarely a horrible potential) that finally a nuclear war will not occur, since a good God would not let humanity be practically if not completely destroyed. Such an argument seems incredibly naive in the face of the extent of the immensely "incredible" outbreak of collective absurdity, the reassertion of the abysmal chaos, in the Jewish Holocaust and in the use of the atom bomb at Nagasaki and Hiroshima. Humanity is indeed capable of— and indeed seems bent upon, or at least seems to be drifting toward—mass self-annihilation. Such an argument (that nuclear destruction will not occur because a good God would not allow it) is also based on a very strange, indeed outlandishly arrogant, assumption that the earth exists for humanity's sake—that is, that the earth itself and other creatures on the earth, and in shallow and deep space, have no place in God's own design apart from human beings.

Whereas, in fact, it may very well be that God will allow humanity in its relative autonomy to go only so far in the mistreatment of its fellow creatures, precisely because the earth is *also* the object of God's love and has its own place in the purpose of creation.

In saying this, I am aware of employing a redefinition of God's omnipotence, and of working with an understanding of God's self-limitation in the very act and process of creation by which God gives relative autonomy to humanity. I am aware that this in turn involves a redefinition of God's immutability, for in this view, God's self-limitation in the act and process of creation means that God's benevolent purposes for all creatures may be foreshortened and taken through a route of suffering. This would all be interesting cosmological speculation were it not for the hard way of God's being for us as deliverer in the person of the crucified eternal Word.[18] The goodness of creation may involve the cost of allowing one portion of creation which is bent on destroying and using up the rest of the earth to follow its willful madness to the extremity.

Such a dread-full scenario is not inevitable, and such speculation cannot become for the ecclesial reality a kind of stoic apathy by which to accept with as much dignity as possible a foregone conclusion. However, the hope which is an alternative to such apathy arises from the realization that we are called to treat the earth, no less than each other, with love. We are called to a fundamental paradigm shift by which we see our relation with the earth as one of mutual care, mutual nourishing, mutual well-being. The common good extends not just to the body politic and economic but to the body ecological as well. There is simply no such thing as deliverance from bondage and oppression for any human community without the simultaneous deliverance for the co-creature earth. The liberating Word of God humanly speaking occurs to move men and women forward in the process of transforming knowing. The reimagination of seeing the earth as the equal subject of God's love, and as a co-creature with whom we are bound in mutual dependence and caring, is part of what that preaching must evoke in us. One of the crucial motivating forces in the fight against nuclear armament is the realization that the benefit of a just peace for humanity presupposes a just peace for the earth's sake.

VI. The Visible Form of the Liberating Word

Proclamation of God's liberating Word occurs not just by preaching but by the Word in visible form as sacrament. I will cite here only the instance of the Eucharist, which is the liberating Word of God made materially visible through the bread and wine, which by the power of the Holy Spirit become for us a participation in the broken body and shed blood of the new covenant. Yes, the Lord's Supper is a re-presenting performed by the believing congregation. Yes, it is an act of recovenanting to be Christ's body in praise and worship, teaching and action. Yes, it is an act in which we claim solidarity with the rest of humanity whom God is delivering from bondage for joyful service to other humans.[19] But it is even more than that. Christ's special eucharistic presence is also a confirmation of our solidarity, as members of his body, with the rest of creation, including the earth. The bread and wine gathered from the scattered hills remind us not simply of the gathering of God's people from all over; they are also signs of the earth, which is chosen also to be the bearer and expression of God's benevolent, just peace, apart from whose wholeness humanity cannot experience its own wholeness. The reality to which the signs point and in which they participate is *not* the earth unattended. The reality is precisely that incarnate Word by whom all things were made, in whom all things will be recapitulated, and whose humanity was constituted of the elements of the earthly "God-bearer," Mary. The liberating Word incarnate, preached and proclaimed sacramentally, is also the Word for the earth's sake.

5

A Critique
of Dominion Theology

Elizabeth Dodson Gray

I want to challenge us to rethink some current assumptions about eco-justice as an issue for Christians and the churches. I want to challenge the assumption that we already have a perfectly adequate basis for eco-justice preaching in our Hebrew Scriptures and our New Testament. I want to show you why I don't think that's so. Then I want to challenge the assumption that we have in our Jewish and Christian traditions an adequate creation theology. By creation theology I mean an adequate mental picture and conceptual grasp of ourselves, our world, and our relationship to the Creator. And finally I want to challenge the scope of the current issues usually thought of as eco-justice issues. Let me deal briefly with this last one, and then spend most of my time with my first two concerns.

In the call to this conference about eco-justice preaching there was a good list of "eco-justice issues"—hunger, employment, caring for the earth, and so on. All of these are good things, important things. Nowhere was there mention of the women's movement as an eco-justice issue. But think of the enormous women's involvement in the environmental movements, such as those for clean air and stopping nuclear power, in the currents of thought called eco-feminism, in the peace movement and the nuclear freeze movement. Think of Rachel Carson, Helen Caldicott, Randy Forsberg—already almost forgotten as the

author of the idea of the nuclear freeze. Think of
Greenham Common, and you think of women. Think of
Hazel Henderson, **who** began her career as a counter-
economist by working as a mother for clean air. When you
start thinking of specific events, places, people—many in
the eco-justice movement involve women taking unheard-
of roles in challenging male madness over eco-justice
issues. In short, the women's movement is perhaps the
largest movement today for eco-justice.

The reason I am bothered by the invisibility of all these
women activists "as women" is that I hear people talk about
the 1970s as a time of apathy, a time when "nothing was
happening." To those people, the 1960s and the civil rights
movement and the anti-Vietnam War movement was a
time of action, but nothing happened in the '70s. Well,
what happened in the 1970s was the women's movement.
It has taken many forms. And it is usually invisible to men
and to male historians and to our male church. But unless
you can see the women's movement and women's concerns
and organizing skills and leadership and energies and
emerging moral judgment in eco-justice movements rang-
ing from Green politics in Western Europe to liberation
movements in Central and Latin America, as well as in the
economies and politics of developing countries in Africa
and in the Middle East, then you haven't seen much of the
eco-justice movement of today and tomorrow.

Where Are We in God's Creation?

Our sense today of where we are in God's creation is very
different from what it was a century, or even a few decades,
ago. Today we know we live and move and have our
being on a small planet in one galaxy among 193 billion
such galaxies. And we know that, like all that is alive here,
we live on the outer skin of this planet, within a five- to
seven-mile-thick layer ecologists call the biosphere. The
biosphere contains all the biological life-supporting sys-

tems and cycles of the earth, and these systems and cycles keep alive all that grows. That includes us.

But we as Christians, when we are thinking as Christians, have blinded ourselves to much of this. We have been helped in dissociating our sense of self from this biological understanding of ourselves by Christian theologians both past and present who have helped us think that just as far as God is removed from creation, we humans are removed from the rest of creation: we are created in God's image and are spirit. And we get very upset when we are reminded of our biological similarity to mammals or other animals. Our theologians have emphasized God's tran-scendence and our own capacities for self-transcendence and being different from the rest of God's creation. Yes, we are different—in the sense of being distinct and unique as a species. But we are kept alive by the air we breathe and in the other ways we participate in the biosphere, just as much as any of the rest of creation.

Think of our planet as like a gigantic tennis ball that has a five- to seven-mile-high coat of fuzz on it. We exist within that fuzz very much the way the "Whos" did in the Doctor Seuss book *Horton Hears a Who.* We are like the Whos in the fuzz of the tennis ball. And when we talk about creation, when we preach about creation, when we teach creation in our Sunday schools, we never mention important little things like the biosphere and ecological cycles. They some-how don't seem to fit in.

But whether we preach about them or not, whether we are moved to religious awe and wonder before these latter-day burning bushes or not, the creation of God on this planet does everything by the interaction of the carbon cycle, the oxygen cycle, the nitrogen cycle, the hydrological cycle, and about a dozen other cycles or round-and-round processes. What's terrific about these cycles—and about the magnificence of God's design, if you will—is that each part of them takes its essential raw materials from the waste products of other parts of the cycle. Each part then does its special thing, dumps its own wastes, and—in the wonderful mystery of God's ecology—those wastes are precisely the raw materials another part of the cycle needs in order to do its thing. Contemplate a cow in a grassy field and you're witnessing, among other things, a part of the nitrogen cycle at work, for the cow eats the grass and, in turn, the cow provides manure that fertilizes the field of grass. As long as there is rain and the sun continues to shine, then the cow and the grass are good for each other and provide for each other. What you are contemplating is a small ecosystem or community of life and interdependence.

You can see the same sort of thing happening around the process of photosynthesis, the sunlight-into-sugars process that goes on in green plants when the sun is shining. A waste product of photosynthesis is the oxygen you and I breathe. We tend to think that oxygen is always there in the air for human beings to breathe. Economists talk about air and water as "free goods." Free, baloney! Oxygen to breathe is there only because it is breathed out by all the green things on the planet, from the blue-green algae in the ocean to the plants and trees of tropical rain forests and the ivy growing on your windowsill at home. In the miracle of photosynthesis, plants, when the sun shines, breathe out oxygen to us. We in turn breathe out carbon dioxide back to them. Once again, it is a never-ending cycle of cooperative community or relationship. We and the plants are totally dependent on each other, each to breathe out so the other can breathe in. But most of us don't feel a sense of community with the trees outside or the blue-green algae in the ocean; we don't have the faintest clue that we can breathe only because plants and trees are breathing too.

Life in Human Society

Now consider how differently things usually go within the circle of human activity. There is energy coming in that we use, which usually someone dug up from the biosphere in the form of a fossil fuel (actually fossil sunshine, stored from photosynthesis long ago). Within this circle of human activity there are also metals and minerals coming in, many of which we also dig up, such as copper and zinc, from the earth's crust or seabed.

What happens to our wastes? Keep in mind now that we're speaking of the contrast between our ways and those of the biosphere. The more our human populations increase, the more wastes we are likely to pour out, and the more the pace of our economic system picks up in growth, and the more and the faster our wastes go back out into the systems of the biosphere—into the air, into the streams, into the soils, into the oceans—until like a house with an inadequate septic-tank system it can't handle so much so fast. The capacity of biospheric systems to use these wastes is overwhelmed.

Members One of Another

Look outside your window and you just see plants and buildings and trees and sidewalks and sky. You don't see ecosystems because you have not been trained in ecology. Most of us haven't. But what is really out there are these communities of life that scientists call ecosystems, in which the wastes of one part of the ecosystem are essential raw materials that other parts of the system need. It's all interconnected and it is all mutually interdependent, and it does its thing and keeps on going indefinitely.

Now about 1942 we got the great idea of producing DDT in the laboratory to get rid of malaria. It was a good thing to do, a great idea: DDT knocked out mosquitoes that carried malaria to humans. But you can't knock out mosquitoes with DDT without also knocking out all the insects you expose to DDT. So you killed all the insects in an ecosystem, and pretty soon Rachel Carson wrote *Silent Spring*, calling attention to how DDT had killed off the food for the birds or, alternatively, how you had poisoned the birds because they ate the poisoned insects.

For a while we thought this was all we had done. But

DDT is a persistent pesticide, what today we'd call "non-biodegradable." DDT is washed by rain into rivers and lakes and oceans. Little fish who feed on algae also get DDT with supper, and the DDT stays in their flesh. Then the little fish and their DDT is eaten by bigger fish, who in turn are eaten by still bigger fish—and the DDT gets "biologically concentrated" and is stored in fatty tissue. In three species—the bald eagle, the peregrine falcon, and the Pacific pelican—the DDT from a fish diet ends up, scientists have learned, in the liver of the female bird, where it interferes with production of an enzyme which determines the thickness of the shell of the eggs the female lays. So for the first time in evolution mother birds laid eggs and sat on them—and the eggs went splat because the shell wasn't thick enough.

Now the point here is not just one of concern for these three endangered species, though we should be concerned, but that we are regularly producing substances in the laboratory and the chemical plant—and we do not have the faintest idea what ripple effects they will have upon our larger life-support systems.

How Did We Ever Think We Could Get Away with It?

When you really get into this, you begin to think there is something really bizarre about the way we have treated the planet. I argue in my book *Green Paradise Lost* that our view of our place in creation came to us as part of our Judeo-Christian tradition. Our whole Western civilization with its science and industrial system is built upon this cultural foundation and is still very much shaped by it. What's been taken for granted in this heritage and in our heads is conveniently summarized by an illustration from a curriculum developed by the Educational Development Center in Newton, Massachusetts. The accompanying text reads: "People in the Old Testament believed in only one God who created a divine order [i.e., hierarchy] that placed people above nature and gave people dominion over the fish of the sea, the fowl of the air," and so on.

What that creation theology from the Bible translates into is a set of relationships we hold in our heads and which we have been deeply socialized into. I've found it useful to diagram those relationships like this:

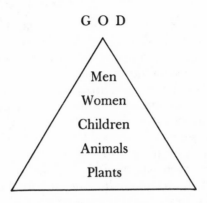

G O D

Men

Women

Children

Animals

Plants

N A T U R E

Note first of all that this is a hierarchy being diagramed here. By that I mean it is a picture of diversity being "ranked." It depends upon the illusion that there is some magic standing point you can take and then, according to your values, say this is higher and more important and of more value than that. What is of highest value is always visualized by us as "up." God is up, above, lofty, high and mighty, and so on. And what is of next value is arranged below. I think you see this most clearly presented in Scripture not in the Genesis accounts of creation but in Psalm 8, which says:

> When I consider thy heavens, the work of thy fingers,
> The moon and the stars, which thou hast ordained;
> What is man, that thou art mindful of him?
> And the son of man, that thou visitest him?
> For thou *hast made him a little lower than the angels,*
> And hast crowned him with glory and honor.

Thou *madest him to have dominion* over the works of
   thy hands;
Thou *hast put all things under his feet*:
All sheep and oxen,
Yea, and the beasts of the field;
The fowl of the air, and the fish of the sea,
And whatsoever passeth through the paths of the seas.
                                      (Psalm 8:3–8, KJV)

What we're given here is a nifty little snapshot in which
God is above, highest in value. Angels are next and just
slightly higher than humans. Then come humans. And
everything else is underneath our feet.

And it's not just that these are of higher worth and value
but that all things and all creatures in this great ladder of
things are supposed to obey their higher-ups. Man and
creation are supposed to obey God, or else. Women are
supposed to obey men, and children are certainly supposed to obey their parents and obey God. Most of us call
pets and other animals subhuman—not nonhuman—and
we assume we can train animals, torture them for our
medical experiments, do horrible things to them as we
raise them to be our food. We can relate to cats, dogs,
horses in terms of personalities with consciousness. They
are at least more like us. But plants I don't think we can
relate to at all. They're simply rooted in the ground in one
place. What in this context we call "nature" is finally on the
very bottom of this pyramid of value and obedience and
who-is-supposed-to-adapt-to-whom.

Paul Santmire, who wrote *Brother Earth,* has said that in
Christian theology nature has been a theological non-
category. It has had all the importance of the stage—or
wall or floor; nature is simply the context in which the
really important thing, the drama of salvation, takes place
between man and God.

Three Myths

What I'm saying is that we have embedded in our heads
this pyramidal picture of our place in creation, and we

confront nature with three myths. The first myth is that *reality is hierarchical.* If there's anything I want you to understand, it is that reality is an interrelated system. A system is something in which everything affects everything else. Most of us don't have a clue what that means, so instead we conceptualize reality in hierarchies.

The second myth is that *man is "above" nature in dominion* or control. Once again, this is rooted in our Judeo-Christian tradition. It is very clearly said in our biblical creation tradition that God has given us dominion, rule. Dominion is a kingly metaphor, and just as God is king in the heavens, we're supposed to reign, in God's name of course, here on earth. And the earth is supposed to obey and adapt to what we say and do. Presumably we're supposed to listen to God up there and only do what God says we should down here.

But the whole mental picture is wrong because nature is not below us, is not awaiting our commands, and is managing itself very nicely unless we go around messing it up.

Let's talk about stewardship at this point. There is considerable effort nowadays to whitewash our tradition and avoid taking a look at what is really happening in the Old Testament and in our hierarchical theological tradition. We are attempting to say that dominion is all right as long as it is done with stewardship. We think our problem has been that we've done it wrong because we made "dominion" into "domination." We did it wrong and tomorrow we'll do it right. That is a fantasy!

We won't do it right, because we don't know enough to do it right. If there's anything I've learned, it is that we don't know enough of the intricacies of the way things work always to do it right. Whether it is DES or EDB or DDT or Love Canal or TMI or AIDS or genetic engineering, we are discovering every day new little intricacies we didn't know existed yesterday. Stewardship assumes we have perfect knowledge as well as a desire to do right by the planet. I don't think we've got either the knowledge or the desire, because we still in our gut feel we're above and we do not have to fit in.

I talk about "fitting in" when people say, "What do you want to substitute for dominion?" My answer is "attunement," or fitting in. That means you've got to listen. It's like what I consider good parenting to be—cybernetic. It means being guided by information feedback: you do one thing tentatively and you wait to see what happens. You monitor it very carefully (which we do not bother to do). If it looks like it's not doing well, you pull back and you change your behavior, trying something else. Attunement means listening, it means adapting yourself. It means fitting in. And it will never be done by us as a culture unless we, as a culture, realize we are not above. We are not going to do that, I don't think we are, until we Jews and Christians take a hard honest look at what we have received from our tradition. Or until we as a culture become more secular, more distant from our religious tradition.

The third myth is that *nature is feminine,* as in "Mother Nature" and "virgin resources." That, at least, did not come from our religious tradition. On the contrary, our creation mythology in Genesis 1 and 2 worked very hard to rule out all attempts to say the original creation of the world had anything to do with female sexuality. If you've compared Genesis with earlier creation myths of the ancient Middle East, you know that's true. Genesis was a polemic that said there's simply no way the procreation by women in bringing new life into this world had anything to do with the creation of the world, the creation of people.

It's not accidental that in Genesis Eve is born out of the body of Adam, the body of a man, which is the reverse of what happens in real life. That is no accident, just the way the only starring role allowed to women practically in the entire Old Testament is Eve in the creation, bringing evil into the world. That's no accident either. But the idea that nature is feminine does not come to us from this religious heritage. It comes to us in other ways. But it is nevertheless very firmly ensconced in our heads and in the ways we function toward nature, even without all that religious legitimation.

Our problem is not that these are myths, because I think humans always create myths, mental capsule-accounts which are simplifications. The problem comes when your myths are so out of touch with reality that you're functioning as though you were on angel dust, PCP, which convinces adolescent children they can swim when they can't, and they jump into swimming pools and drown. Or that they can fly, and they hurl themselves off buildings trying to. Myths that are so incongruent with the facts of life on our planet are a danger to your health. Hierarchical myths in an interrelated planet are dangerous to your health, and to your future.

Darwin's Revision

When Darwin wrote *The Descent of Man*, the biblical pyramid of hierarchy (now called the Scale of Being) still shaped his thinking. To say that our real ancestors are related to monkeys is to drop us four steps down in the biblical hierarchy.

The evolutionary paradigm turns out to be exactly that same hierarchical pyramid, except that we've removed the action of God from the top. Evolution instead begins from the bottom in the primeval soup, and we envision ever divergent evolution as going up the levels from lower (simpler) to higher (complex) species, with humans occupying the top place. A hundred years after Darwin, Jacob Bronowski could turn the whole thing over in his book and television series entitled *The Ascent of Man*, and it remained believable. Why? Because the mental picture in our heads really hadn't changed, even though we thought we'd undergone an epoch-making transformation of thought.

We have confused our human uniqueness with our being superior. *Biologists view every species as unique.* A bioecological perspective views the human species as unique also, but not necessarily as the most important or the most adept. Certainly we don't have the best ears or the fleetest feet or the keenest sense of smell. We don't even have the largest brains, nor can we echolocate as do the dolphins. And we would be hard-pressed to show that what humans do is as important or as foundational to all life on this planet as what green plants do in photosynthesis.

The Role of Illusion

Attitudes like this coalesce into a pervasive "anthropocentric illusion," as I named it in my book *Green Paradise Lost*. We have seen only ourselves at the center of value and significance in God's creation. This assessment of our place and value in the scheme of things has been the basis of our Western science and technology, and it is going to kill us unless we abandon it. What I am suggesting is nothing less than that we finish the Copernican revolution. It felt theologically and religiously cozy to us to believe that we were at the center of the skies and that the sun and everything else went around us. All that is what Galileo and Copernicus overturned. When they discovered that what we see in the skies—our astronomy—requires a different assessment of the earth's place in the order of things, with difficulty we adjusted our astronomy. But we left in place the mental picture of a pyramid. We were still on top and therefore we could continue to do what we pleased.

Several centuries ago we adapted to a different astronomy. Today we must adapt to a different picture of our place in the orders of value and priority and importance of things. The diversity of this planet does not exist to be ranked. To ask of any differences, male/female, white/black, human/tree, Which of us is better? is to ask a dumb question, when viewed from the perspective of ecology and an understanding of systems.

Ranking Diversity: The Core Issue

My contention, spelled out in more detail in *Patriarchy as a Conceptual Trap,* is that this ranking of diversity has come from patriarchy. Very early in human existence males created patriarchy because they as males did not produce life out of their bodies the way women did. In our early days as humans I don't think we understood how women managed to do that and what the male role in that was. Out of that male insecurity, I think males created a culture in which what men do is valued more and what women do is valued less—in short, patriarchy. It's a culture shaped to reassure males that they are terrific.

My problem with such a culture is that once you start ranking the primal difference between male and female and asking, Which of us is better? you then develop a mind-set that's always ranking things that are different or varied or diverse. Now, today it is almost impossible for us who have been deeply socialized into such a culture to encounter diversity—other humans or other species—and not immediately ask, Which of us is better? Which of us is smarter? Taller? Richer? More beautiful? Stronger?

So ultimately the problem of patriarchy is conceptual. It involves a fundamental mistake in how we think and organize what we perceive. What I want you to understand is that you are not going to deal with the problems of eco-justice until you deal with patriarchy. And what I find distressing again and again is that nowhere in the eco-justice dialogue and writings—except for what I say—is there any sense that patriarchy has any relationship to the eco-justice set of issues. When I say that ultimately the problem of patriarchy is conceptual, I mean that the problem which patriarchy poses for the human species is not simply that it oppresses women. Patriarchy has errone-ously conceptualized and mythed Man's place in the uni-verse. And thus, by the illusion of dominion that it legiti-mates, it endangers the entire planet.

6

Process Theology
and Eco-Justice

W. Kenneth Cauthen

I

Let me state my thesis initially in the strongest possible terms: Process theology is better suited than any currently available alternative for uniting eco-justice concerns with biblical faith. Moreover, it generates basic images useful in preaching which are credible, relevant, and emotionally powerful.

Process theology is important not only in and of itself but also as a contribution to what I believe is a potential and emerging outlook which is being elaborated from many different points of view. A major paradigm shift is underway. By this I mean a comprehensive way of perceiving, conceiving, and believing which we are invited to help bring to birth. The new vision exists as a possibility arising out of the actualities of the present, but it lures us forward to actualize it in thought, feeling, and action. The evidences of this evolving worldview are appearing in the natural sciences, in the social sciences, in psychology, and in philosophy. It is beginning to be articulated by physiologists, biologists, economists, ecologists, planners, systems analysts, anthropologists, political scientists, futurists, and visionaries.[1] My grasp of this vision is partial, fragmentary, and vague. I could be guilty of overestimating its reality, its significance, and its future. I will proceed to describe it as best I can, knowing full well that I may be mistaking a ripple in my mind for the wave of the future.

The new vision centers in an intuitive perception of systems or organized unities. Key words are holistic, unitary, synergy, harmony, cooperation, and synthesis. It speaks of energy flow, of interdependent networks, of dynamic connectedness, of apposites rather than opposites, of organic processes capable of creative transformation. It sees nature and biological structures as providing both the foundations and the limits of human possibilities. The focus is on total systems, thought of as dynamically interacting, mutually sustaining parts which work together to support the functions and goals of the whole unit. Reality is viewed as a complex organization of interdependent systems. Its key insight is the interconnectedness of things. Contemporary science tends to see nature at its fundamental levels as made up of dynamic, organic systems, of organisms with lifelike characteristics. Nature is constituted by patterns of energy that act like living systems in which parts and wholes mutually influence each other. The materialistic, deterministic, mechanistic, atomistic physics of previous centuries is gone. Certain features of dynamic-organic systems described in contemporary scientific models of the world can be found at every level of reality from the subatomic to the global ecological level. Human individuals are best seen as members of one another, having a genuine autonomy but organically related to the total natural, social, and ultimate environments in which they live and have their being.

Process theology in particular makes use of insights and categories provided by the philosophies of Alfred North Whitehead, Charles Hartshorne, and others as a way of formulating a biblically based theory of God, the self, the world, and history.[2] The usual result is a theocentric theology united with a Logos Christology. The New Testament witness to Jesus of Nazareth is typically seen to be the clarification and exemplification of patterns, purposes, and possibilities that are found throughout the cosmos and that give the clue to the meaning and destiny of human life.

The central category of process philosophy is life. It is a "philosophy of organism."[3] According to this metaphysical vision, the world is made up of value-seeking events or units of experience which have the characteristics of freedom, intentionality, and organic unity which we associate with life or organisms. Reality, then, is a social process in which these life events are organically connected to everything else, especially to those neighbors nearest in time and space. The whole cosmos is constituted by a complex hierarchy of interrelated series and societies of these occasions of value-seeking experience. At the base of all things is a Creative Power and Purpose who is the source of both order and novelty in the world. The universe, then, is pervaded by aims, meanings, and values undergirded by a quest for self-realization experienced as enjoyment. The most important fact about the world is the sense of worth, the intuition that something matters, the feeling that bedrock reality is the urge toward goodness and beauty.

This dynamic, organic, teleological, theistic worldview has a number of advantages to offer to theology, as well as to society at large. Let me mention three.

1. A philosophy of organism can overcome the long-standing dichotomy in modern Western thought between nature and history or, to put it differently, between cosmic facts and personal values. It is not necessary here to go into detail about the mechanistic, deterministic, and materialistic cosmology which for three centuries seemed to be the unavoidable implication of modern empirical science.[4] According to this view the world is made up of tiny bits of dead, purposeless matter moving and developing in accordance with mathematically exact and inexorable laws. The result of this view was a dualism between physical reality and personal purpose, between nature and history. A good deal of modern philosophy can be seen as the attempt to overcome this bifurcation between the world of fact and the world of value—a dualism which has been prominent in much post-Kantian Protestant theology in both its liberal and its neo-orthodox forms. "Scientific

materialism," as Whitehead called it, is suitable neither to philosophies based on the reality of freedom, meaning, and purpose as ingredients in the universe itself—nor to the outlook of twentieth-century physics. Process philosophy provides a way of unifying the world in which the quest for personal values is seen to be the exemplification of patterns and purposes found throughout the whole cosmos and grounded in the intentionality of God.

2. Process theology provides a basis for uniting biology and politics in a comprehensive worldview. It is just this sort of integration that eco-justice presupposes as its foundation. If biology is the science of life, and if politics deals with the way human beings organize themselves in quest of justice and the good life, then I take eco-justice to involve a union of these concerns. Eco-justice devotes itself to the achievement of a globally sustainable society which can provide a sufficiency of goods and services conducive to the good life within a framework of justice for all. My own interest in what I was then calling biopolitics was kindled in the late 1960s when I became aware that it was necessary for theology to enlarge its vision to include our relationship to nature as well as our concern with social problems. At that time I wrote:

> It is imperative not only that nations learn to live in peace with justice for all but that we also learn how to relate ourselves to our natural surroundings in such a way as to stay alive and prosper. We cannot afford to continue to make war, to tolerate oppression, to allow the gap between the rich and the poor to persist. But neither can we indiscriminately and indefinitely plunder the planet for its resources, overpopulate it with people, and pollute our air and water without paying the terrible consequences in human misery. If we are to have a future at all, we must at least learn the elementary requirements of biological survival.[5]

At that time I called for an ecological model for theology. I would reiterate that call today as being even more urgent than ever before.

Process theology is especially suited to provide such a model. It has at its center a vision in which the central aim of God is to create and to promote the enjoyment of life in all its myriad forms, including not only persons but all sentient beings whatsoever. To advocate biopolitics, which aims at preserving life and enhancing its fulfillment within the constraints of justice, is to align oneself with what is deepest in bedrock reality itself. To live eco-justly and to promote the ends of eco-justice is to live in tune with God. The very aim and substance of process theology is the development of a conceptual model which can bring together modern science, biblical faith, and the politics of life into an integrated whole based on a worldview which is rationally sound and emotionally satisfying.

3. Process theology can account for and interpret the global interdependence which is a central fact of our time. It is commonplace today to speak of the interconnectedness of the whole human family within the totality of the whole network of biological systems which generate and support all forms of life. Life is a seamless web of connections, of mutually supporting systems and parts. Increasingly there is a world economy, so that major fluctuations in any large component have implications almost everywhere. Intercontinental missiles are the symbol of the global context of politics. What happens in Moscow, Washington, Peking, Managua, and Beirut has worldwide implications. The burning of fossil fuels around the globe may have consequences for the world's climate which will affect every continent. Elaboration of the details of the interdependence of the ecological, economic, political, and cultural facts of life in our time is unnecessary. It is a part of the conventional wisdom of our age. Process theology is based on a vision centering around the interconnectedness of all things. It is an organic-relational philosophy of life. Its deepest insight is that reality is a social process. Hence, it is admirably equipped to account for and interpret global interdependence in all its forms and levels. The very image of Spaceship Earth vividly represents this fact in a symbol

which in itself embodies the interconnectedness of ecology and technology. My claim is that process theology can provide valuable contributions to an operating manual for Spaceship Earth in its perilous but yet promising journey into the future.

II

Let me turn now to interpret some more specific themes of process theology relevant to eco-justice preaching.

The Goodness of Creation

According to process theology there are no "vacuous actualities,"[6] that is, no valueless entities, no dead matter. The world is made up of units of experiencing, pulses of life aiming at satisfaction. In the strictest sense reality consists of nothing other than experiencing subjects who are capable of enjoyment. An experiencing subject capable of enjoyment is intrinsically valuable, that is, good in and of itself. Understood this way, the idea of the goodness of creation is taken in the most literal way. The created order is constituted in its entirety by occasions of living experience which are good in themselves and which aim at the good.

It is true, of course, that objects exist as well, such as rocks, typewriters, mountains, and oceans. Common sense tells us, and process theology agrees, that such things have no subjectivity. They are not experiencing subjects. Rather they are aggregates composed of occasions of experience. Hence, pure objects as such have only instrumental value, although the units of which they are composed do have some, but relatively little, intrinsic value. Objects may, of course, have instrumental value for human beings or animals or both.

It is important to add that there is a hierarchy of value among living beings. The value of organisms increases as the range and depth of their capacity for enjoyment increases. Jesus said that sparrows and sheep are valuable, but a human being is worth much more (Matthew 10:31; 12:12). Process theology affirms the same principle and offers a metaphysical basis for the judgment. Value is measured in terms of the richness, complexity, and intensity of feeling enjoyed by organisms. Human beings have a much wider and deeper capability for enjoyment than animals and hence have more intrinsic worth than they, though all life has some value. I stress this point because I have had some rather intense arguments with some eco-justice–minded theologians who contend for what seems to be a pure democracy of value in which the claim of superior worth for people is regarded as a prejudice of Homo sapiens. Let me just say that I find the notion that a mosquito has the same value as a human being simply incredible and without foundation in either Scripture or reason. Reverence for all life, yes. Equal reverence for all life, no.[7]

The Redemptive Activity of God in Nature and History

According to process theology, every organic event is an aim at value. Whitehead said that every living being is driven by a threefold urge: to live, to live well, and to live better.[8] This universal eros is the quest for self-realization experienced as enjoyment. It is found as well in God, who is the chief exemplification of the urge toward creative advance in quest of richer and fuller realizations of value. The role of God in this process is to lure the world forward toward more complex configurations of harmony and intensity which increase meaning and satisfaction. Events are driven from behind by efficient causes which exert causal influence, but they are drawn from above and ahead by final causes in the direction of a larger good. God exerts persuasive power on the world in the form of ideal possibilities offered for choice. God acts creatively and redemptively in every event and in every configuration of events involving free agents calling all life forward toward greater realizations of justice and joy.

Ethics as Response to God's Creative Purpose

Process ethics, as I espouse it, can be stated philosophically or theologically.[9] Put in philosophical terms, the foundation for morality can be expressed in a twofold way: honor intrinsic value in persons and in all sentient beings (the deontological imperative) and promote self-realization and enjoyment in persons and in all sentient beings (the teleological imperative). Put in theological language, the equivalent formulation would be as follows: Reproduce in your actions toward others the quality and aim of God's creative and saving action toward you. The quality of divine action is defined by love (agape). The aim of divine action is the actualization of the commonwealth of God (the kingdom). Hence, the fitting response to God is to love one's neighbor as oneself and to allow and facilitate the coming of the commonwealth of God on earth.

This ethical perspective results in a theory of justice centering in the theme of self-realization in community. In this view justice is to society what health is to the physical body. The individual organism and the social order may ideally be thought of as interdependent networks of mutually sustaining activities which work together to support and enhance the functions and goals of the total system. A just society is, in this sense, a healthy society. In my perspective the aim of justice is to increase or to maximize the welfare (happiness, enjoyment, self-realization), the freedom, and the equality of all persons within the constraints that each of these three factors exerts on the others. Tensions arise of course, in this outlook, as in all systems, between the good of the whole society taken as a unit and the rights and well-being of individuals. The final referent must be to individual people, because they are, in the strictest sense, the only subjects of experience. Yet in a secondary sense we can speak of the good of the group which may sometimes take precedence over the claims of some individuals, as when we send certain people off to war to defend the country for just reasons. Moreover, some social orders are healthier or better than others in that they facilitate a more nearly optimum balance between the good of the whole and the self-realization of individuals. And within that framework other judgments have to be made about which arrangements best balance the rights and welfare of some individuals and groups in comparison with other individuals and groups.[10] Justice, as we all know, is a complex and difficult norm and goal. The best we can hope for is an approximation that will be filled with ambiguities, compromises, and trade-offs.

In short, responsible living consists in responding to God in gratitude for the gift and promise of life by seeking to knit together organically the potentials for enjoyment found in all living beings, especially persons. So to respond and so to attune one's life to the aims of God in nature and history is to permit and to enable the coming of the commonwealth of God in which justice and joy are universally actualized.

While space does not permit the development of a doctrine of human nature and of sin, it can easily be seen what form a theory of evildoing might take. Sin is, in essence, the opposite of and any deviation from the norms of human motivation and action that have been stated. Irresponsibility before God and neighbor refers to acts which dishonor the intrinsic value of other persons and which do not count the good of our human companions equal to that of the self. Sin also defines the total state of being, the gestalt of character, in which irresponsible motives reside and from which wrong actions proceed.

I believe that a theology oriented around such themes as I have suggested, but only briefly developed, catches up major motifs of the biblical witness. I also am maintaining that such a theological point of view is admirably suited to the concerns implied by the concept of eco-justice. This outlook has its vulnerabilities and weaknesses, as do all human formulations of the gospel. Since the critics of process theology are ever ready and willing to point out these defects, I will concentrate on making the positive case. Finally, I contend that process theology is relevant to the task of preaching geared to further eco-justice aims. Let us examine this in detail.

III

Process theology on its technical and theoretical side may seem remote from the practical task of preaching to people in intelligible language. Yet out of it can be generated concrete images that are vivid, credible, relevant, and evocative. Process theology can be translated into ordinary language that both conveys its vision of the world and grasps the mind and imagination in emotionally powerful ways. It is preachable in ideas and images that can illuminate issues and motivate people to effective response to the good news. Process theology makes use of organic symbols. Its concepts center around an understanding of experiencing subjects. Life may be taken to be its central organizing motif. I want to lift up two metaphors generated by process theology which may be useful in preaching related to eco-justice concerns.

The first metaphor may be put as a question: What is history pregnant with? From time to time right and ripe moments emerge which offer the potential for significant human advance toward greater justice and happiness. These occasions are produced by objective developments in the historical process. They come about because of a particular confluence of events which creates the possibility of novel advance, of a positive transformation in human affairs. History becomes at certain times and places pregnant with new possibilities of life, of justice, of enjoyment. Such a pregnancy occurred in the eighteenth century, which gave birth to the Declaration of Independence and the Constitution of the United States. Another pregnancy occurred in the nineteenth century which led to the overthrow of slavery. Another possibility of new birth came about a generation ago which gave life to the civil rights movement epitomized by Martin Luther King. Significant change is most likely to occur in the presence of a perceived threat when positive alternatives are available as a result of a fresh vision of human possibilities. A major portion of moral responsibility consists in discerning the signs of the times which point to moments pregnant with new life.

With respect to eco-justice I believe that a certain fullness of time may be at hand. We are experiencing a threat to global life as we approach the biological limits of the earth in terms of population pressures, natural resources, and pollution. Ecological disaster is a real potential. The other major threat to the human future is, of course, the possibility of nuclear war. These threats are actual. Are positive alternatives available? I believe the eco-justice movement is an attempt to respond to these demonic threats with a hopeful vision of an alternative future that can be actualized *if* we are willing to meet the conditions that its birth imposes on us. This is both positive and hopeful. I believe that history may indeed be pregnant with two possibilities. The first is a way of believing that is required and possible for survival and salvation in our time. We need an organic philosophy of life, an eco-justice vision, which I believe process theology can help to develop. The second is a way of living required and possible for survival and salvation, an eco-justice morality which honors the intrinsic value of all life and promotes the enjoyment of all life in an organic system of global interdependence. We need directives that will lead to the achievement of a sustainable society in which the imperatives of justice and the promotion of the enjoyment and ecstasy of life are guiding norms. Theology and preaching are challenged to help find ways of uniting biology and politics into concrete policies which can help bring about the birth of a new age with which history is pregnant.

The second metaphor follows from the first. Our task as

citizens and believers is to be midwives of the common-wealth of God. The human task is not to be Atlas bearing the heavy burdens of the world. Instead we are to be midwives facilitating the birth of new possibilities of justice and joy. The pregnancy is an objectively real potential in the events of the time. We are called upon to discern what is happening, what might happen if we don't act or act foolishly, and what could happen if we act wisely. God is luring us by the power of ideal possibilities to catch a vision of what the future can be if we repent and believe the good news (Mark 1:14–15). History is pregnant with new life. Can we learn soon enough and well enough to be midwives of the commonwealth of God by which we allow and facilitate the birth of a new age? Are we willing to try?

That, I believe, is the challenge lifted up before us by an eco-justice vision of life. Preaching informed by the insights and inspirations of process theology can contribute to the art and science of midwifery that is required to bring to life the possibilities of justice and joy with which history is pregnant.

7

Eco-Justice Themes in Christian Ethics Since the 1960s

Roger L. Shinn

Eco-justice is a word that I have not found in any dictionary. In appearance it is a hyphenated term: a linking by artifice of two concepts. That is a sign of much that has gone wrong in our history. It points to a drastic bifurcation, a theological heresy, a cultural schism—all of which require us to patch together what a demented world has torn apart.

I. A Biblical Perspective

In Scripture the words that we sometimes translate "justice" have to do with God and the divine creation, with human relations and with animals and with the garden in which God set man and woman. Scriptural justice has something to do with that "Christian materialism" described by William Temple when he insisted that Christianity is "the most avowedly materialist of all the great religions." Its "most central saying," he affirmed, is: "The Word was made flesh [*sarx*]," a term "chosen because of its specially materialistic associations."[1]

In the Bible the Sabbath and the sabbatical year are for animals and the land, as well as for people. The whole earth is full of God's glory (Isaiah 6:3). The psalms bid all creatures to praise God. The sea, trees, mountains, living things testify to the divine majesty (Psalm 148). The awe for animal life is so deep that when God authorizes Noah and his descendants to eat flesh, they are not to consume blood (representing the "life" of the animal). God, says Jesus, is concerned for the lilies of the field and the birds of the air.

I realize, of course, that Arnold Toynbee, Lynn White, Jr., and many others have made the argument that biblical monotheism robbed the world of divinity and made it available for human exploitation. White, especially, has put the case in an exquisitely phrased and subtly nuanced form. We need to listen to his accusation: "Especially in its Western form, Christianity is the most anthropocentric religion the world has seen. . . . By destroying pagan animism, Christianity made it possible to exploit nature in a mood of indifference to the feelings of natural objects."[2] It is helpful to hear his eloquent appeal to recover something like the sensitivity of St. Francis to God's creation all around us. We might note here that René Dubos responded to White by suggesting that the Benedictines offered a better example.[3] Francis loved God's creatures, but had no ethic of production. The Benedictines sought to establish mini-economies that were ecologically sound, even though the words ecology and eco-justice had not been invented.

White's declaration had a special force when he issued it at the 1966 meeting of the American Association for the Advancement of Science. It was a time when several formulations of theology, with marvelously inept timing, were exulting in human technological prowess and the Christian "desacralization" of nature, just before the new sensitivity to the ecological crisis showed the thinness of these theologies.

But I won't grant White his whole case. It was the Greek philosopher Protagoras who coined that anthropocentric claim, "Man is the measure of all things," a boast unimaginable from a Hebrew prophet. It was Aristotle who said that, since nature does nothing in vain, "the inference must be that she has made all animals for the sake of man. And so, in one point of view, the art of war is a natural art of acquisition, for the art of acquisition includes hunting, an art which we ought to practise against wild beasts, and against men who, though intended by nature to be governed, will not submit; for war of such a kind is naturally just."[4] Can you imagine an apostle talking like that?

Perhaps we can hear the Lord responding to Protagoras, "Can you bind the chains of the Pleiades, or loose the cords of Orion?" (Job 38:31). A space age makes that logic only more impressive. Or maybe we can hear the Lord reply to Aristotle, Do you really think the hawk, the eagle, Behemoth, and Leviathan were put here for you to eat or make into pets?

It was the Romans, not the Hebrews, who "treated the natural environment as if it were one of their conquered provinces,"[5] who after the Punic wars plowed salt into the soil of Carthage so that vegetation would not grow there, who (as a British chieftain said, according to Tacitus) "make a desert and call it peace."

Against this mood of conquest the psalmist says that God, not we, stretched out the heavens like a tent. Yes, God gives plants that we may cultivate "to bring forth food from the earth, and wine to gladden the heart" (Psalm 104). But it is not for human utility that God made the stork and the wild goat, the badger and the lion. Why is Leviathan in the sea? For our convenience? No, "to sport in it."

II. The Modern Heresy

The sources of our modern problems are far more diverse than the Bible, stemming more from rejection of biblical monotheism than from heeding it. We are doing what has often been done before—threatening a civilization by combined exploitation of natural environment and exploitation of people—but on a scale never achieved before. The modern world does it with a special virtuosity, for which there are cultural sources.

There are the Greek and Roman roots, which I have already mentioned. There is ordinary human irreverence and arrogance, often attacked by Hebrew prophets and poets. There is the more distinctively modern dualism of Descartes, separating mind from body and mechanizing all of nonhuman nature. There is the quantification of values, springing out of the creative discovery in the seventeenth and eighteenth centuries that mathematics is a clue to more than people had realized, then fallaciously making it the clue to practically everything.

Add to these sources a predatory technology and industry, not entirely evil in intent, sometimes in fact liberating for some people, but too often arrogant and inhuman. Add the illusion of Adam Smith that the division of labor and competition are the keys to unlimited productivity and that self-interest is really the best way to serve the public interest.

All this and much more led to that flashing economic spectacle following World War II, an era that E. F. Schumacher described to the British Council of Churches in these words: "There have never been twenty-five years like this before, and there may never be twenty-five years like this again."[6] Walt W. Rostow headily described "the stages of economic growth," with the expectation that all societies, provided they met a few conditions, could take the economic growth of the most affluent societies as models for their own practice.[7]

Christians began to think that they had been misled in their traditional emphasis on modesty in desires, on conservation of goods and resources, on restraining their own wants for the sake of sharing the world's goods. Was it not their duty, some asked, to spend and consume, thereby stimulating employment and a rising standard of living?

The National Council of Churches, through its Department of Church and Economic Life, undertook its studies of "the affluent society"—a title taken from John Kenneth Galbraith's famous book.[8] That study, I am happy to say, saw the problems in affluence: the injustices in distribution of wealth, the "pockets of poverty" in the midst of wealth (although in global terms it would have been more accurate to talk of pockets of wealth in the midst of poverty). It recognized the illusions of human self-sufficiency and of confidence in economic success as an answer to human need. But it did not—as I, who was part of the process, must confess—have much ecological sensitivity.

The promise of economic expansion led to a new version of "the liberal dream."[9] The gap between rich and poor—both the gap in American society and the gap between the rich nations and the poor nations—had always been an offense (or at least an embarrassment) to a people with some remnants of a biblical faith and some memories of an egalitarian Declaration of Independence. The offense was not so great that the society was ready to do anything radical to overcome it. But now a new possibility appeared: to overcome the gap, not by demanding sacrifices of anybody, but by making everybody rich.

As Walter Lippmann described the political genius of Lyndon Johnson's "war on poverty," the program did not require sacrifices from anybody—as Franklin Roosevelt's earlier attack on "economic royalists" had seemed to do. Johnson's program was to be financed from "the growth dividend" in the economy. And by extension, international economic development promised relief of poverty for the poor on a global scale. Liberal church people largely joined in. They acclaimed secularization, the demystifying and desacralizing of nature, the triumphs of human ingenuity, thus setting themselves up (as I have already suggested) for the criticisms of Lynn White and others.

The conventional liberal wisdom, which had criticized the Eisenhower administration for letting economic growth lag, hailed the Johnson administration's hopes for the benefits of economic growth—until these turned sour with the war in Vietnam. In 1966, when Consolidated Edison was under attack for not expanding sufficiently its production of electrical power, its chief executive officer, Charles Luce, made a remarkable speech at the Interchurch Center. He argued that there was no way that the New York metropolitan area could continue to double power consumption every decade, as it had been doing. The religious professionals challenged him, urging many remedies, including increased use of nuclear energy. He sounded a little lonely as he insisted that conservation must be a major part of any program for the future.

But an awakening was imminent. It came in many places—in the churches, in scientific thinking, in the culture at large. The problem of eco-justice was about to get attention.

III. The Awakening

An early herald of the awakening was Joseph Sittler's address to the New Delhi Assembly of the World Council of Churches in 1961. Sittler emphasized the theological importance of "the care of the earth, the realm of nature as a theater of grace, the ordering of the thick, material procedures that make available to or deprive man of bread and peace." That joining of human need with care of the earth might be taken as a definition of eco-justice, although the word had still not been coined.

Sittler invoked biblical theology: "Our modern view of nature as by definition not having anything to do with the divine is in complete hiatus with the Old Testament view. There nature comes from God, cannot be apart from God, and is capable of bearing the 'glory' of God."[10] I might add that, as Sittler well knew, there is no word for nature in the Old Testament, which speaks of the creation. We human beings are part of that creation. In it, we—who are made of dust but made in the image of God—have a distinct responsibility; but we are creatures.

Sittler's speech won great acclaim, largely (I'm reluctant to say) because of the beauty of his prose. There was no immediate programmatic response to it.

In the United States, Kenneth Boulding alerted the National Council of Churches to ecological issues in 1966. In a paper prepared for the Committee on Church and Economic Life, then reprinted widely in this and another version, he pointed to the disastrous consequences of reckless economic exploitation of resources and called for an economy appropriate to life on "Spaceship Earth."[11] Although his paper made a big splash, it evoked no immediate programmatic response. Instead, the National Council of Churches soon let its Committee on Church and Economic Life die, due to preoccupation with other issues, most notably racial injustice. The mistake was not concern about race; it was failure to relate racial problems adequately to the issues of ecology and economic justice.

That same year, 1966, was the year of the World Conference on Church and Society, convened by the World Council of Churches in Geneva, Switzerland. Its theme was "Christians in the Technical and Social Revolutions of Our Time." Although Boulding was there, his ecological interests got little attention. The conference was more adept at talking about social revolutions than technical revolutions, but its recommendations called for the churches to give more attention to the social meaning of technological change. The long-term result was that the World Council of Churches initiated some major programs on social justice and a smaller program on science and technology.

When the Working Group on Church and Society undertook its studies on technological change, it barely guessed what was about to happen. An explosion of ecological concern, manifest in scientific organizations and the United Nations, called for attention from the churches. In the World Council of Churches the ecological interest never became detached from the commitment to social justice, but it called for rethinking the remedies for injustice. A series of international meetings culminated in the World Conference on Faith, Science and the Future at the Massachusetts Institute of Technology in 1979. Among the lay specialists who participated in various stages of that study were Margaret Mead, the American anthropologist; Jørgen Randers, the Norwegian scientist and coauthor of the first report to the Club of Rome; Charles Birch, the

Australian biologist; as well as Boulding, Schumacher, and White. Equally important were the contributions of Eastern Europeans, Africans, Asians, and Latin Americans who, although not household names in North America, brought to us indispensable and often painful insights into the process.

As the studies concentrated on a variety of issues— energy (including nuclear energy), genetics, food, population, warfare and weaponry, economic inequality, transfers of technology from one society to another—debates were frequent, often intense.

IV. The Great Debate

The central issue in the debates concerned the relation of the new ecological concerns to the old issues of social justice. Is there a basic conflict between ecology and justice? The question came up in hundreds of contexts around the world. Arguments flared in secular and in religious circles.

To the poor, both in the United States and around the world, the new attention to ecology often seemed to be a fad, one more evasion of the issue of social justice. To people bored with struggles over civil rights and economic injustice, ecology offered a diversion. It became the fashionable and glamorous topic. Or still worse, it sometimes seemed that the ecological jag was actually part of a conspiracy against the poor. They wanted to reply: "You rich have mounted the ladder of economic success and dangled before us the hopes that we could follow you. Now you want to kick over the ladder that you told us to climb. After getting yours, you say that the world's resources are too limited for us to get ours."

As victims of past injustice expressed their anger, some eco-enthusiasts volunteered for the role of villains. The Paddock brothers advocated the calculated neglect of the most desperate countries and regions in order to concentrate attention on those that had some better chance of

pulling out of their poverty.[12] Garrett Hardin proposed
"lifeboat ethics" by which the favored societies, like ship-
wrecked passengers on a lifeboat, would preserve themselves rather than rescue the drowning people who wanted
to clamber into the boat, thereby sinking it.[13] Critics were
right in attacking the elitism of such beliefs. The same
critics often missed another point made by the Paddocks
and Hardin: international economic aid, as actually prac-
ticed, often does more harm than good. That point was
part of the radical criticism of Frances Lappé and Joseph
Collins,[14] whose argument, contrary to their intentions,
was often welcomed by the complacent and lethargic
people who wanted to do nothing about world hunger and
poverty.

The specific arguments sometimes centered on population. Bucharest in 1974, it happened, was the scene both of
a World Council of Churches consultation on technological and ecological concerns and of a far larger United
Nations conference on population. The World Council,
because of a history of conversations in which some mutual
trust had developed, avoided the worst collisions of the
United Nations, but both meetings heard a familiar argument. The industrialized nations saw rising populations as
a major cause of world poverty. The "Less Developed
Countries," in United Nations jargon, located the cause of
poverty in victimization of the poor by the rich. Sometimes
both sides argued from dogmatic positions uninfluenced
by any openness to data that might challenge the dogmas.
Eventually the debate shifted somewhat because China,
which had once held that population was no problem for a
Marxist society, began a strenuous program to control
population growth.

Nevertheless, ecology often seemed to be the hobby of
the privileged. The lovely calendars of the Sierra Club
rarely hung on the walls of slum dwellings. When industrialized countries saw the importance of reducing pollution, poor countries replied that they would be glad for
some industrial pollution. In the United States, when

environmentalists advocated fewer and smaller automobiles, auto and steel workers wanted more manu-
factured.

The poor and their advocates often argued that economic advancement for impoverished people was most
likely in an expanding economy. The more ethically sensitive environmentalists replied that their polemic was not
against the poor but against life-styles and economic structures that actually victimized the poor. But the poor were
unconvinced. Their experience usually persuaded them
that more and better jobs came with rising prosperity.

The discussion in the churches sought to transcend
dogmatic opposition between ecologists and advocates of
justice. The concept of eco-justice implies that the two
interests are interdependent. Ecological concern actually
heightens the importance of social justice. By destroying
illusory answers to the problem of injustice, it increases the
urgency of more fundamental answers. High productivity
and the trickle-down theory of wealth are not now working
well. Poor people have always known that a lot was wrong
with such theories. Now more people are finding out. Both
hard necessity and ethical concern demand answers more
radical than the conventional clichés.

To say that is easy and, I believe, valid. But to implement
it is hard. To show that a problem is harder than the world
once thought may be a good thing; it may stir efforts for
fundamental change rather than palliatives. But the same
logic may encourage defeatism or resistance. One negative
response is, If the problem is that tough, I may as well give
up. Another negative response is, If the needed change is
really radical, I'll resist it. Those responses set an agenda
for the churches.

V. The Need for Change

There are signs that the world is in for changes that
nobody can entirely foresee. There is no way of knowing
for certain the social consequences of the coming exhaus-

tion of petroleum, of shortages of water and other precious resources, of disposal of toxic wastes. Human ingenuity will overcome some specific problems, usually at an economic cost and at the risk of producing new problems. Other problems will require the human race to live with an awareness of limits that was characteristic of most human societies through the millennia but that was briefly forgotten by a few North Atlantic societies in the era of the industrial revolution.

Thus it is logically ridiculous and morally irresponsible to assume that China or India or most of Africa and Latin America can ever consume automobiles or beefsteaks at the rate that the United States now consumes them. It is highly problematic to think that the United States can consume at such a rate for another century—or that the people of the world will contentedly watch such consumption.

To confound the problem, the dominant capitalist and socialist ideologies are alike bankrupt in facing the problem. Both emerged in the industrial revolution and shared assumptions peculiarly characteristic of that time.

The classic formulation of Adam Smith assumed virtually infinite capacity for production. The division of labor was the key to productivity, and the market was the ideal mechanism of distribution. There were no basic ethical problems in society—save the necessity for a few agreed-on rules of the game, such as the protection of life and property along with the keeping of contracts—because self-interest and public good were assumed to coincide under the beneficent "invisible hand." The gap between rich and poor was tolerable, because the system of production was so effective that everybody benefited from it. If there were shortages, rising prices would guide consumption toward other products. As to pollution, such "externalities" barely figured in the system. As to population, that problem was still awaiting Malthus and his gloomy answers.

Today there is not a country in the world that operates on the basis of that economic philosophy. And many countries are trying, by one device or another, to preserve fabrics of international finance and credit that cannot survive the present stress in the system.

Marxism, because it assumes that capitalists limit production to what is most profitable, promises to produce more than capitalism. In the *Communist Manifesto*, Marx and Engels say that the proletariat will "centralize all instruments of production in the hands of the state" and will then "increase the total of productive forces as rapidly as possible." Soviet power plants carry the slogan from Lenin, "Communism is Soviet power plus the electrification of the whole country." Apparently in Lenin's thought the electrification deserved priority. In 1920 he said: "You know that electricity is the basis, and that only after the electrification of the entire country, of all branches of industry and agriculture, only when you have achieved that aim, will you be able to build for yourselves the communist society which the older generation will not be able to build."[15]

It would be surly in the extreme for Americans to begrudge electricity to the rest of the world. The relevant point is that Lenin's idea of communism depended on a productivity that is still economically and ecologically beyond the reach of many, many people. In fact, world electrification now looks farther off than it did a few decades ago, when energy resources seemed unlimited. It may be that new forms of solar conversion will someday make electricity available virtually everywhere; that remains to be seen.

One thing we know is that most of the human race lived and died before anybody had electricity. I have no desire to return to the preelectric era; I see neither virtue nor pleasure in trying. But I know that some people have lived glorious lives without electricity, and I am sure that the joy of living is not proportional to the electricity consumed.

The example proves little. But it suggests that our era may require a re-visioning of human possibilities for which neither capitalist nor communist thinking have prepared us.

VI. What We Can Do

It should be evident that I do not have a world plan for the achievement of eco-justice in this generation. I do not see anybody who does have a persuasive plan. But there are things that we can do. The possibilities are in two areas.

The first is personal life-style. Every individual can reconsider his or her way of living, with the aim of modifying some extravagant or destructive habits.

For some people this is the activity of greatest hope. Donella Meadows, coauthor of *The Limits to Growth,* the famous first report to the Club of Rome, now puts her emphasis there. Four years after publication of the book, after she had thought through the many criticisms of it, she reconsidered its theme. She reaffirmed its major contentions but said that if she were rewriting it, she would put greater emphasis on redistribution of the world's goods. And she had shifted her hopes from a great world plan to the voluntary acts of individuals learning new and simpler ways of enjoying life.[16]

I have two problems with that reasoning. One is that the structure of our society makes high consumption necessary for many people. Many a poor family has to maintain two cars or lose income and become still poorer. Institutions lock people into costly and extravagant styles of living. The second problem is that voluntary changes in life-style make only a tiny difference unless many, many people adopt them.

Even so, changes in life-style are important. A big part of the resistance to change and of the dynamics of international conflict is the desire of people in many places to maintain costly life-styles. A change of life-style is a token of integrity, a step beyond talk to action. Furthermore, a discipline accepted voluntarily and at some inconvenience has consequences in consciousness-raising. People who participate in an Oxfam-sponsored day of fasting perceive the world differently toward the end of that day. And if they contribute the cash savings to relief of hunger by direct aid or through political channels, they nudge the world a little way toward a healthier future. So there are good reasons for churches to commend to their members reconsideration of personal life-styles.

The second possibility is structural changes. They are coming, whether we like them or not. Many of them will be involuntary. I expect that they will be costly, that they will involve suffering, that there will be (as there already is) violence. The more they are influenced by human understanding and concern, the more chance there will be for peaceable, voluntary, even joyful change.

What structural changes can we advocate? Here our ignorance is great. We might work toward a better organized world, a more internationally interdependent world, a greater sharing of the world's resources. Or we might seek a more decentralized world where "small is beautiful" and local economies are largely self-sufficient. Or we might look for some combination, now unanticipated, of big-scale and small-scale institutions.

With such uncertainties, churches had better not be dogmatic. If they claim to know answers when they actually do not, they irritate rather than help the situation. Part of their message had better be a call to ethical exploration.

But that does not mean that there is nothing worth doing until new answers appear. If we do not yet see the grand scheme, we can see many actions of moral responsibility. I suggest not a comprehensive list but a few examples.

This is a time to recover the traditional biblical ethic of moderation of consumption, an ethic that for a brief fragment of modern history seemed obsolete. Conservation of energy is one case in point. Many corporations and home dwellers have already, under the pressure of "the bottom line," taken big steps in this direction. Still greater steps are necessary. When people join moral concern to financial pressure, they often see new possibilities.

This is a time for worldwide emphasis on public health, on education, and on participation of people in the social processes that influence their lives. Such steps—not exotic and not destructive of resources—have their own worth, and they have an interesting consequence. Usually they contribute more toward the voluntary moderation of population growth, another important goal, than single-minded attacks on the population problem.

This is a time for "technological assessment" and "social audits" of industrial processes. These new terms have entered the public vocabulary for good reasons. Technological assessment sometimes shows that unintended damage from a new technology outweighs intended gains. Social audits show that some innovations, although they bring profits to some, inflict costs on the public at large. For example, government policies sometimes encourage new industrial efficiencies at the cost of unemployment that becomes a public liability; a social audit might lead to a change in policies.

This is a time for deciding who should pay for the "external" costs of production. If an economic organization pollutes the air and water or causes acid rain, it is "externalizing" (transferring to the public) some of its costs of production. Sound environmental protection policies require producers and consumers of goods to pay the costs, not inflict them on bystanders.

This is a time for tax policies that help people meet basic human needs rather than subsidize lavish living. It is a time for Research and Development directed toward life and opportunity for all the people of the world, not toward the enhanced profit of the already wealthy.

This is a time for intense examination and action on "technology transfers" among the nations. When industrialized nations transfer technologies to the less developed countries, the major consideration is too often the benefit of the sellers of the technology, not of the country buying it. The result too frequently is a widening gap between rich and poor societies.

This is a time, above all, for urgent efforts toward world peace. The issue of war and armaments is far too portentous to get only a paragraph in a discussion of eco-justice.

But war, along with everything else that is to be said about it, remains the most ecologically destructive of all human activities. And international economic and development policies, guided by military motivations, are a damaging blow to that combination of concern for ecology and justice that we call eco-justice.

Such examples, stated so briefly, sound platitudinous. Each of them, when thought through, has momentous concrete implications for personal, political, and economic decisions in this suffering, threatened world.

VII. Issues for Preaching

The opportunity in preaching on eco-justice is, most fundamentally, the opportunity in all preaching: to evoke awareness and response to God's grace and judgment in human life and history. But the particular qualities of contemporary history present peculiar opportunities and problems.

Usually people (including preachers) do not give attention to a problem until they feel its pressure. When they feel the pressure—in this case the pressure of injustice, of protests against injustice, or of ecological peril—they are likely to get "uptight" and resist creative responses. When the pressure relaxes, they relax into complacency.

An example is the "energy crisis." The critical shortages of petroleum in recent American life brought out the worst in human behavior as people panicked, fought each other in gasoline stations, and demonized oil-exporting countries. Even so, society learned from the situation and initiated some genuine economies in consumption. But later came the talk of a "petroleum glut," new habits of self-indulgence, and a common belief that the energy crisis had been phony.

These temporary aberrations are deceptive. In twelve years the price of petroleum at the Persian Gulf increased by a factor of 28.[17] Increase the price of anything enough, and there will be a market glut. But there is no talk of petroleum glut in China and in India, the two largest countries of the world, or in Tanzania and Bangladesh and other poor countries. There is no more petroleum on earth than there was at the time of the "crisis," and new explorations have for the most part been disappointing. The seeming glut hides the realities. One task of preaching is to raise to visibility realities that are not obvious.

The theological content of preaching on eco-justice is, to a surprising extent, "the old-time religion." That does not mean mere repetition. Preaching, even when preachers repeat themselves, is always reinterpretation. But the reinterpretation for today requires a recovery of some themes of the traditional gospel, often with a new urgency and a new relevance. The church needs to hear and to tell that

   • We cannot serve God and mammon. (Many of us thought we had outmaneuvered God on that proposition, but we are learning our error.)
   • People live by bread—the Christian "materialism" of William Temple still has a meaning for us—but not by bread alone.
   • The love of money is still the root of all kinds of evil, not the healthy dynamism that will bring full employment and happiness.
   • Sharing is important to the meaning of life.
   • The biblical concern for justice, especially the concern for the poor and oppressed, is as authentically important today as at any time in human history.

In particular, our era has the opportunity to reappropriate three traditional doctrines in their uniqueness and their interaction: the doctrines of creatureliness, of stewardship, and of dominion.

To understand creatureliness is to realize that we human beings did not create and cannot dominate this universe. Life is a gift. The creation around us is a gift, to be enjoyed responsibly, not recklessly exploited.

To understand stewardship is to realize the radical

character of this doctrine. There is no such thing as private property—or, for that matter, government property—in any absolute sense. "The earth is the Lord's." Property arrangements are sometimes a ratification of power of possession, sometimes a useful way of sustaining a social order without constant violence. In either case they are only a tentative assignment of what is not finally ours. Within this mysterious cosmos some part of earth is a garden entrusted to us "to till it and keep it" (Genesis 2:15).

To understand dominion is perhaps most difficult of all. After hearing all the tirades that have been uttered against that doctrine for its destructive consequences, I want to say a good word for it. Christian faith affirms a human dominion—a reverent, creaturely dominion, not a renunciation of dominion. To appreciate dominion is to accept freedom, foresight, and power—and to exercise them responsibly.

When gypsy moths destroy a local ecosystem, nobody holds them morally accountable. They are simply being gypsy moths. Lacking freedom, foresight, and the kind of power that follows from freedom and foresight, they lack dominion and responsibility. Human beings have the competence to behave morally or immorally.

Our generation has seen some good examples of human dominion. The apparent elimination of smallpox is a case in point. I am not reluctant to affirm a hierarchy of values in which human life outranks the smallpox virus.

I am grateful for the increase of human life-expectancy from 47 years to 73 years in the United States in the period 1900–1980.[18] I am grateful that life expectancy of 53 years in India now surpasses the life expectancy of nineteenth-century European nobility,[19] that life expectancy in the Punjab has risen from 23 years in 1900 to 55 years now.[20] I know that the value of life is not measured in years, but to value life is to rejoice in the decline in infant mortality.

The reduction of infant mortality has brought other problems to the human race. But I would rather meet them with a further exercise of dominion than to release those stocks of smallpox virus still preserved in a very few laboratories.

Barry Commoner has made the old saying "Nature knows best" into a "law of ecology."[21] I don't believe that. To those who assert that nature knows best, I must ask, Best for whom? For human beings? For an unconscious ecosystem? For God?

I know that we human beings have been too brash, too reckless, too destructive in our misuse of power. But Christian faith is not the renunciation of power. It is gratitude and responsibility. It includes reverent dominion, along with a sense of creatureliness, a radical stewardship, a commitment to justice for all God's children on this earth our home.

8

Preaching for Creation's Sake: A Theological Framework

Dieter T. Hessel

The preceding chapters probe some of the outmoded assumptions of a dying culture while helping us to discern the movement toward distributive justice and environmental renewal in the new creation. They equip us to comprehend, celebrate, and contribute to God's shalom purpose in history and nature even as we listen to creation's groans. Those groans result from the crushing burdens placed on poor people and the brutal treatment of nonhuman victims by modern society. The previous pages have a cumulative effect of reforming our consciousness regarding the crisis of ecology and justice even as they invite our participation in fresh dialogue and action for eco-justice.

The hyphenated word "eco-justice" means the well-being of all humankind on a thriving earth. Eco-justice occurs where human beings receive sufficient sustenance and build enough community to enjoy harmony with God, each other, and nature, and where the rest of creation is appreciated not simply as useful to humanity but as valuable to God. Such a comprehension of eco-justice sharpens our theological insight and fosters our critical social analysis even as we move to clarify ethical norms for responsible action. The eco-justice crisis challenges us to become faithful, informed, engaged people who really mean "Thy kingdom come, thy will be done, on earth as it is in heaven."

I. The Preacher's Dilemma

If North American society is experiencing another "time of trial" in which a period of history hangs in the balance or is pregnant with new possibilities,[1] then our ministry at such a crucial transition requires something more than thinking and acting as usual. Precisely in this situation ministers of the Word confront a pastoral and personal dilemma. How shall we respond to the many pew sitters who would just as soon *not* hear any prophetic echo of creation's groans or any delineation of the outmoded assumptions of a dying culture? Classic psychological mechanisms of denial, anger, and bargaining that come before acceptance of terminal illness are operating among the majority in our social system and churches. "Don't tell us we can't grow our way out of social and economic problems! Where would we be without the technological conquest of nature? How can a freedom-loving way of life and a church which is doing good be under divine judgment?"

Many church members prefer that preachers respond to their own groans as perplexed, hassled, or frightened people who try to live responsibly and want to believe in progress. They seek inspiration and solace in order to function better at work, school, or home, and in community groups. Not only do they have an unwritten contract with us that stipulates delivery of a comforting word; they pay us out of surplus wealth or investment earnings which reflect some personal success within present socioeconomic arrangements.

Meanwhile the public and its representatives have taken a flight from reality—denying major problems rather than tackling them constructively. Quite a few politicians, business leaders, and preachers continue to extol that old-time religion of salvation through (economic) growth and to picture a rosy future despite contrary evidence. While deliberately ignoring major threats to the environment and the plight of poor people, our leaders "heal the wound of

God's people lightly by preaching 'Peace, peace!' when there is no peace" (Jeremiah 6:14). Major Protestant and Catholic bodies have at least continued to advocate policies of distributive justice and moved in solidarity with communities burdened by poverty, unemployment, and pollution. But few in church and society have come to grips with the possibility that prevailing socioeconomic theory and practice bring "nonprogressive change"[2] instead of genuine historical progress for the good of all creation.

If in this setting we are to "fuse the biblical horizon of eco-justice with our socioeconomic horizon,"[3] and to proclaim the Word of God rather than to offer comforting religious chaplaincy, then something basic is required of us. We preachers are called to make words once spoken among the faithful and written in biblical scrolls speak now with grace and truth so as to empower repentance—personal, ecclesial, and public. It is our responsibility to show what the vision of shalom, the covenant of justice, and the ministry of the Messiah mean for us in today's world.

To the extent that we fulfill this responsibility we can expect to be resisted by the prosperous and ridiculed by false prophets (cf. Jeremiah 28). Our preaching for creation's sake is likely to be viewed as unrealistic, out-of-style, or downright subversive of this disobedient and dying culture. Yet from the deeper perspective of biblical theology, eco-justice is the only faithful realism, the only depth perspective on the wrenching changes we are experiencing. Dare we believe that preaching with this perspective will enable people to hear and respond to the liberating Word of God, to witness to the spirited power of the biblical vision for created life, and to act as loving stewards in all personal, economic, ecological, and political relationships?

To carry out this mandate requires our public engagement and theological reflection. On the one hand, we cannot comprehend the crisis apart from eco-justice analysis and action. On the other hand, we cannot grasp or teach

an adequate social ethic for these times apart from biblically grounded theological reflection. Here I want to focus
on a theological framework that is crucial to the reformation of eco-justice ministry.

II. Fresh Theological Affirmations

Can we restate our theological affirmations in a catholic
and reformed, rather than merely revivalist, way? Preaching that follows an individualistic revival model would first
convict, then convert. It emphasizes how awful were our
lives and deeds, and then revels in our rescue by God from
this worldly mess.

The social version of this same preaching style paints a
terrible picture of our dire systemic situation and then
seeks to convince us that by God's power behind our will,
we can change things. If this social approach is ethically
responsible in contrast to the political fatalism of personal
revivalism, both kinds of revivalism fail to plumb the depth
or appreciate the prevalence of human sin in systems and
selves. Neither conveys the power of the kingdom vision,
the cost of God's reconciling grace, nor the difficulty of
loving justly in a world of "forced options."[4] Revivalism in
all its forms tends to reinforce conventional moralism and
accommodate to culture more than transform it.

The biblically grounded alternative is to begin with the
good news of God's whole work in creation and to let that
illumine our situation. Toward that end an important
systematic theology insight I would pass along is that only
in the light of God's faithfulness do we even recognize the
pattern and depth of human sin, or the service to which we
are called. The light of God's presence in the world enables
humanity to discern shalom and to recognize sin. These
depth understandings are not derivable from social con-
vention or habitual religion; they are revealed by the
ultimate Source of life. Both shalom and sin are known
within the faith relation initiated by God who is Creator,

Liberator, Judge, and Reconciler—the God of biblical testimony and of contemporary experience.

Eco-justice consciousness and action are quickened primarily by encountering the power of God's work throughout creation, not merely by piling up terrible facts of injustice to people and nature, however shocking. Since much of our institutionalized sin results from socioeconomic achievement, not from individual human weakness, transformative preaching needs to begin at a revelatory starting point that illumines the predicament of the powerful and privileged. More will be said about modern sin under the second point below.

Following are some expository comments on a brief statement entitled "Our Theological Understanding" which was debated and affirmed in January 1984 at a Toronto Consultation on Acid Rain. The consultation brought together denominational representatives with scientific as well as theological expertise from twenty-five Canadian and United States church bodies.[5] The group's theological affirmations were first drafted by William E. Gibson and then amended and affirmed in a plenary session in which I also participated. The five points, reproduced in boldface type below, when taken together, offer a contemporary framework for theological reflection and eco-justice preaching, to be informed by public engagement and study of the other chapters of this book.

1. God as Creator of heaven and earth and all earth's creatures looks lovingly upon all the works of creation and pronounces them very good. God continues to care for creation and to fill all the creatures with good things.

This first biblical affirmation, echoing the Genesis story, deserves careful contemplation, as does the creation itself. The affirmation reflects God's delight in the creation as a totality of environment and creatures to whom good life is given. God is creation's lover. Nature and history are designed to cohere in the creation which God loves and continues to care for. The divine intention is to seek the well-being of humankind with all creatures on a thriving earth.

What then is the fitting human response to the gift of creaturely life? It is to rest joyfully in and to care lovingly for this delightful garden and for each other in a manner consistent with God's pleasure. Divine enjoyment of the whole process of creation becomes the model for good work within community, the goal of which is to enhance and to enjoy relational harmony with God, others, and nature within history.[6]

As Roger Shinn reminds us, the Sabbath and sabbatical year highlight this purpose of rest, enjoyment, play—the need to celebrate and restore relational harmony which observes the rights of animals and the land as well as the rights of people. Thus we acknowledge God's purpose in the web of life. We respond appropriately to the Creator by expressing trust, reverence, gratitude, service. Our life in human community in the midst of nature has the *prospect* of shalom. "Where shalom exists, there we enact our responsibilities to one another, to God, and to nature. But shalom is more than that. It is fully present only where there is delight and joy in those relationships."[7] Or as Kenneth Cauthen puts it:

> At the base of all things is a Creative Power and Purpose who is the source of both order and novelty in the world. . . . The most important fact about the world is the sense of worth, the intuition that something matters, the feeling that bedrock reality is the urge toward goodness and beauty.

There is no romantic illusion in this theological definition of reality. Although the fullness of God dwells in and unites all things (Colossians 1:19–20), our planet and culture never were and are not now perfected, but are in the process of becoming whole. God cries out like a woman in travail determined to birth a new humanity (Isaiah 42:14–16). The new creation is still developing or being born, waiting with eager hope for liberation (Romans 8:19–24).

2. God as Deliverer acts to protect, restore, and redeem the earth and its creatures. These have become co-victims with all humanity, victims of the sinful pride and greed that seek unwarranted mastery over the natural and social orders, and the sinful sloth and carelessness that refuse responsibility for understanding and serving God's world.

Creation is not mere stuff to be mastered and used for human convenience. Creation, we have already seen, is the divinely purposed harmony of created being, to be cared for *fittingly*.[8] Modern society under the sway of the Protestant ethic and the spirit of progress, both Smithian and Marxist, has read human "dominion" in terms of remorseless mastery rather than reverent caretaking.

Instead of shalom, we experience the modern world as victimized—a montage of social oppression and ecological ruin interspersed with technological marvels which only benefit a minority of the world's people. Particularly involved in suffering are the earth and its creatures, along with oppressed human groups. True, *all* humanity is victimized by the modern idolatry which "practices [economic] growth as a good of unquestioned and ultimate worth. . . . [But] our situation is not merely that we are all dominated by the idol of growth; it is also that certain *groups* of persons are exploitatively dominated by other groups of persons"[9] because of *pride and hierarchy*.

Elizabeth Dodson Gray would emphasize that the poor and nature are brutally dominated through *patriarchal* mastery of natural and social orders which become institutionalized and are fed by common greed. This mastery, of course, is unwarranted by the Creator, who acts to deliver. Part of creation's process of liberation, notes E. David Willis, is that neither nature nor history sits still under oppression. Precisely because God takes creation's side, the earth and humanity will not remain in perpetual bondage.

One might say that c eation fights injustice and resists

oppression by moving toward ecological disaster as well as social revolution or a threatening economic crunch. Most obviously, this is a revolt against those who have misused technological, economic, and political power to manipulate nature and to control people for profit. More broadly, creation's revolt is directed against the greed and sloth of prosperous people in each national security state who benefit from current socioeconomic arrangements.

Modern society has depended on an unrealistic but religiously held belief that nations can grow their way out of unemployment, urban and rural deprivation, class-race-sex domination, budget and trade deficits—in short, that justice to present and future generations can be finessed by an economics of rapid growth. Policies that would curtail polluting and oppressing growth are strongly resisted, because they contradict this article of faith of political economy. When it comes to issues of eco-justice, we are a stiff-necked people in the same sense in which the prophets applied the term to the Israelites. They forgot their liberation from slavery in Egypt by the power of Yahweh, who covenanted with them at Sinai so that they could illumine and serve God's loving justice. Stiff-necked people reject both the message of judgment and the vision of hope underlying eco-justice because neither judgment nor hope is congenial with the way things are. We who preach for creation's sake must confess our own complicity in this sinful condition. Along with those who have the most power to control and hoard resources, we too are dominating others and exploiting nature, while the oppressed wait expectantly for justice (Psalm 146:7f.).

3. God as Jesus Christ has acted to reunite all things and to call the human creature back to the role of the steward, the responsible servant, who as God's representative cares for creation and acts in society for the sustenance and fulfillment of the one human family.

Messiah Jesus incarnates the loving justice of God and revives a whole covenant faith that has spiritual power and

sociopolitical reality within nature.[10] Jesus expresses unequivocal love for the world and the whole human family,
and shows solidarity with the oppressed, filling the hungry
with good things and sending the rich empty away (Luke
1:53). Jesus identifies his ministry with the Deuteronomic
code of justice and the Levitical jubilee year. In so doing
Jesus highlights the right of all creatures and human
beings to sustenance, and the responsibility of all human
beings for stewardship.

By sustenance is meant the right to food, clothing,
shelter, a healthy environment, and health care. Many
people in Jesus' day and in ours have had these rights
violated, though they are at the center of the biblical
covenant ethic of justice. Then as now, the peripheral
nations and sectors of societies are being impoverished of
necessary resources of sustenance and used as dumping
grounds for toxic wastes. The meek seek only sustenance
while the rich treat their environment as a mine and sewer.
Jesus asserted human sustenance rights in his teachings
and healings, his action in the grainfield and temple. Yet
our society remains uncertain about everyone's social right
to sustenance, comparable to the other civil rights of
freedom, protection, and voice. Today we must reassert
every human being's right to have "social arrangements
that will reasonably ensure our sustenance in the face of
ordinary, serious, and remediable threats."[11]

To ensure sustenance rights and the environment to
sustain them is the primary role of responsible stewardship. The English word "steward" is our translation for the
Greek word *oikonomia*. Hence stewardship is *oikonomia*, a
word that also means the management of a household.
In the words of William E. Gibson, during remarks at
Toronto:

> The purpose of economics is not the maximization of produc-
> tion or of profit, because that may be bad stewardship, destruc-
> tive of earth's continuing fruitfulness. The purpose is provision
> of sufficient sustenance for all. . . . Stewardship in economics

means making arrangements, constructing and maintaining a system, under which each person according to his or her gifts of talent and ability participates in the work of meeting the needs and enriching the life of the household. Each member contributes to the common enterprise; each has or receives enough for health and fulfillment. But since the household functions after the fall, the social arrangements have to be such as to restrain the power, pride, and greed of any who would appropriate more than their fair share of the goods available, or who think they are the absolute owners of the materials they control so that they can do whatever they please without concern for the other members and without accountability to God.

This, of course, requires that we "alter our own expectations; until we have ceased to demand of Earth more than our just share of its bounty, . . . so that the majority of Earth can be brought to more humane levels of existence," as Douglas John Hall concludes in his definitive study *The Steward*.[12]

4. The Creator-Deliverer acts in the ecological-social crisis of our time to demonstrate that same divine love which was manifested in the cross of Christ; and we as a covenant people are called to increase our stewardship, in relation both to nature and to political economy, to a level commensurate with the peril and the promise with which God confronts us in this crisis.

The previous reference to God's reuniting all things in Christ and this affirmation of the divine love manifested in the cross underscore the power of Christ, "the creating, enlightening, life-giving Word enfleshed," to overcome alienation toward each other and the earth. As we are made "one body through the cross" (Ephesians 2:16), the sacramental presence of Christ in bread and wine confirms "our solidarity as members of his body with the rest of creation including the earth"[13] and our creaturely dependence on common elements of sustenance. The crucified Lord confronts us with the peril and promise of human life in creation. The One who was humiliated and resurrected shows how much God suffers with all co-victims, particularly the poor and the earth, and God's power to inaugurate the new creation.

God covenants with us to participate in this stewardship. Therefore, we can respond commensurately with care for all creaturely neighbors and with action to facilitate the coming of God's commonwealth on earth. Stewardship of the new creation involves humanity in creation's suffering and renewal. We become God's hands in doing unfinished liberating work, the outcome of which remains both perilous and promising. Is it too much to say:

> If there is to be any redemption of humanity from evil in the world, it is up to us. We can never again abdicate our responsibility to an omnipotent deity. If God is omnipotent, it is in and through the power of human love. Only if we take humanity seriously on humanity's terms [within creation] may God be delivered, with us, from evil.[14]

5. Human stewardship is not a dominion of mastery. It is a dominion of unequivocal love for this world. It is to be exercised with respect for the integrity of natural systems and for the limits that nature places on economic growth and material consumption.

For us, also, there can be no renewal without suffering, and by us there can be no stewardship that does not serve creation. Our society has hardly begun to face the limits that nature places on polluting economic growth and our material consumption. As nature lashes back to protest human insult, and as the oppressed gain a voice and act for justice, we who would be stewards must decide how to position ourselves—namely, with continuing oppression or with movements to liberate the oppressed. We too must choose whether to ignore or to respect the rights of the poor and of nature, and therefore whether to hate or to love the world of creation.

Belatedly, but with gathering momentum, through covenant groups which support life-style change, and through ecumenical mechanisms at national and regional levels, the church is moving to demystify the political economy and to work for economic and ecological justice. Thus the Toronto statement we have been following concluded:

> As stewards:
> We seek a political economy directed to the protection of the poor and to the sufficient and sustainable sustenance of all people;
> We accept the responsibility of using political processes to check the abuses of power that would otherwise continue to victimize the earth and the poor; and
> We insist that the costs of restoring the polluted environment and of structuring sustainable practices and institutions be distributed equitably throughout our society.

The specific policy implications of this stewardship have to be worked out contextually in light of our values, available knowledge, and democratic pluralism. In the case of acid rain, the churches called for cleanup of sulfur dioxide and nitrogen oxide emissions to a level necessary to protect the health of the continent's most sensitive environments and individuals, and we recommended industrial and pollution abatement/control strategies that are environmentally sound, that preserve existing jobs and create new ones, that protect the poor, and that encourage energy conservation and renewable energy systems.

Working to overcome this and any other serious threat to God's creation will require perseverance, energy, and faith.

III. Questions for Preparers and Hearers of Eco-Justice Sermons

Given the theological framework just sketched, and all that this book suggests about preaching for creation's sake, how do we go about it? It seems unnecessary to summarize here the practical advice offered by the other authors.

Instead, we offer a set of questions for every preacher's consideration in carrying out her or his responsibility to speak words that may manifest the Word in our situation. They were prepared by the planners of the Eco-Justice Preaching Institute in consultation with homiletics professor James A. Forbes.

1. What is the central theme of the sermon?
   a. What theological issue is at the heart of the sermon?
   b. What theological resources besides Scripture does the preacher utilize?

2. How does the sermon take Scripture seriously as a source of God's word to today's congregation?
   a. How does the sermon trace the connection between the biblical "then" and the situation "now"?
      The biblical passage presents an analogous social issue or dilemma.
      The biblical passage emphasizes a Christian social value or virtue which has present application.
      The biblical passage is seen in terms of its strangeness to, or distance from, us in our culture.
   b. How does the sermon overcome familiar obstacles to a fusion of horizons? (See Gottwald.)

3. How does the sermon address current issues of human justice?
   a. What examples of injustice are cited? What information is communicated?
   b. Does the preacher cite a range of experts including victims of current policy?
   c. Is the social analysis and theological theme communicated in a form other than prose in the sermon or the liturgy?

4. How does the sermon indicate awareness of the ecological dimensions of the current human situation?
   a. Repeat questions under 3.

     b. How does it suggest that concern for the nonhuman creation should be incorporated in Christian decision-making?

  5. How does the sermon take account of the situation of the hearers, even as it seeks to listen to the oppressed?

     a. How sensitive is the preacher to the dilemma of the hearers? Of others who are oppressed?

     b. How does the preacher identify with the needs and aspirations of the hearers? Of others who are oppressed?

     c. How does the preacher link the hearers' responsibility to divine judgment and grace? (Look for the yes and no in the sermon.)

  6. What course of action is suggested in response to God's activity within the eco-justice crisis?

     a. What change does the sermon expect of hearers?

     b. What behavior or influence does it project on their part?

     c. Is attention given both to the response of individuals and to that of the congregation?

     d. What ways of acting or educating are recommended, and how do these connect with the congregation's mission and ministry?

  7. What about this sermon helps (or hinders) me in receiving its message?

Sermons that are informed by these questions and by the lively liturgy and communal Bible study of a ministering congregation[15] are more likely to echo creation's groans, speak a liberating word to the church, and invite action for abundant community in a just, sustainable, enjoyable world.[16]

Notes

1. Eco-Justice: New Perspective / Gibson

1. "Liberalism" is the dominant philosophy of the modern era, as given definition in the seventeenth century, notably by John Locke. See Victor Ferkiss, *The Future of Technological Civilization* (George Braziller, 1974).
2. William Ophuls, *Ecology and the Politics of Scarcity* (W. H. Freeman & Co., 1977), p. 8.
3. Ibid., p. 9.
4. See Selected Readings.
5. Norman J. Faramelli, "Ecological Responsibility and Economic Justice: The Perilous Links Between Ecology and Poverty," *Andover Newton Quarterly* 2, no. 2 (1970): 87.
6. Ibid., pp. 89f.
7. Ibid., p. 85.
8. Ibid., pp. 90–92.
9. Donella H. Meadows et al., *The Limits to Growth: A Report for the Club of Rome's Project on the Predicament of Mankind* (Universe Books, 1972). This report is the most systematic presentation of what I have called the limits-to-growth thesis.
10. *Eco-Justice* (Valley Forge, Pa.: American Baptist National Ministries). This is an undated pamphlet, published in 1972 or 1973.
11. "Eco-Justice: The Human Priorities," *JSAC Grapevine* 4, no. 5 (Nov. 1972).
12. But see Herman E. Daly, *Steady-State Economics* (W. H. Freeman & Co., 1977).
13. See Ian G. Barbour, *Technology, Environment, and Human*

Values (Praeger Publishers, 1980), p. 310. Barbour draws on Willis Harman, *An Incomplete Guide to the Future* (Stanford University Press, 1976).

14. See Ronald J. Sider, *Rich Christians in an Age of Hunger* (Intervarsity Press, 1977).

15. See Wendell Berry, *The Unsettling of America: Culture and Agriculture* (Avon Books, 1977).

2. The Biblical Mandate for Eco-Justice Action / Gottwald

1. Hans-Georg Gadamer, *Truth and Method* (Seabury Press, 1975), esp. pp. 258, 333–341. Thomas W. Ogletree, *The Use of the Bible in Christian Ethics* (Fortress Press, 1983), likewise employs "fusion of horizons" as a basic category.

2. Juan Luis Segundo, *The Liberation of Theology* (Orbis Books, 1976), develops the hermeneutical circle at length (see his definition on p. 8). The structure and scope of this hermeneutical conception in Segundo is examined in relation to other common hermeneutical models by Anthony J. Tambasco, *The Bible for Ethics: Juan Luis Segundo and First-World Ethics* (Washington, D.C.: University Press of America, 1981). The term "circle" may be misleading since the image may connote a repetitive movement that gets nowhere, which is not Segundo's view. Some prefer to speak of "hermeneutical circulation" to refer to this dynamic movement toward clarifying and addressing present issues in their biblical and historical depth dimensions. One might even speak of a "hermeneutical spiral."

3. In discussion of my paper at the Eco-Justice Preaching Institute, it was asked if I may not have overstated how widely the Bible is known and how highly it is regarded. I concede that there probably has been a certain decline in substantive knowledge of the Bible and in direct appeal to it. Nonetheless, I calculate that the Bible is more widely known and more normatively, if diffusely, present to consciousness in our society than any other body of tradition (cf., e.g., Northrop Frye's notion of the Bible as "the Great Code" of Western discourse). Exactly how thoroughly or accurately the Bible is known is of course problematic.

4. Here I have especially in mind Bruce C. Birch and Larry L. Rasmussen, *Bible and Ethics in the Christian Life* (Augsburg

Publishing House, 1976); Ogletree, *The Use of the Bible in Christian Ethics;* Tambasco, *The Bible for Ethics.*

5. For orientations to social-scientific biblical scholarship on the two Testaments, see Frank S. Frick and Norman K. Gottwald, "The Social World of Ancient Israel," in *The Bible and Liberation: Political and Social Hermeneutics,* ed. by Norman K. Gottwald (Orbis Books, 1983), pp. 149–165, and Robin Scroggs, "The Sociological Interpretation of the New Testament: The Present State of Research," in *The Bible and Liberation,* pp. 337–356.

6. Norman K. Gottwald, *The Tribes of Yahweh: A Sociology of the Religion of Liberated Israel, 1250–1050 B.C.E.* (Orbis Books, 1979), which builds on, enlarges, and corrects George E Mendenhall, *The Tenth Generation: The Origins of the Biblical Tradition* (Johns Hopkins University Press, 1973). A compact, comprehensive, and judicious statement of "an amended Mendenhall hypothesis," which is close to Gottwald's position, appears in Marvin L. Chaney, "Ancient Palestinian Peasant Movements and the Formation of Premonarchic Israel," in *Palestine in Transition: The Emergence of Ancient Israel,* ed. by David N. Freedman and David F. Graf, The Social World of Biblical Antiquity series, 2 (Sheffield, England: Almond Press, 1983), pp. 39–90. Specifically ecological aspects of the material base of early Israel are treated systematically by David C. Hopkins, "The Dynamics of Agriculture in Monarchical Israel," *Society of Biblical Literature Seminar Papers* 22 (1983): 177–202.

7. Eric R. Wolf, *Peasant Wars of the Twentieth Century* (Harper & Row, 1969).

8. Articulate expressions of this paradigm appear in George Ernest Wright, *The Old Testament Against Its Environment,* Studies in Biblical Theology 2 (London: SCM Press, 1950); idem, *God Who Acts: Biblical Theology as Recital,* Studies in Biblical Theology 8 (London: SCM Press, 1952). For a fuller critique of this dualistic reading of biblical faith, see Gottwald, *Tribes,* pp. 903–913.

9. For elaboration of the implications of my reconstruction of early Israel for political economy, see Gottwald, "Church and State" in *Ancient Israel: Example or Caution in Our Age?* (Gainesville: University of Florida, Department of Religion Lecture Series, pamphlet, 1981). With respect to our ethical

assessment of Israel's social history see idem, "Two Models for the Origins of Ancient Israel: Social Revolution or Frontier Development," in *The Quest for the Kingdom of God: Studies in Honor of George E. Mendenhall*, ed. by Herbert B. Huffmon et al. (Eisenbrauns, 1983), pp. 5–24. Concerning the theological import of the religion and society linkage in early Israel see idem, "The Theological Task After *The Tribes of Yahweh*," in *The Bible and Liberation*, pp. 190–200, and an essay on the Bible in Liberation Theologies forthcoming from Orbis Books in a volume edited by Lee Cormie and T. Richard Snyder. I would also add a trenchant work from an evangelical perspective: Stephen Charles Mott, *Biblical Ethics and Social Change* (Oxford University Press, 1982), which includes biblical theoretical contexts for political reform and political revolution.

10. Willard M. Swartley, *Slavery, Sabbath, War and Women: Case Issues in Biblical Interpretation* (Herald Press, 1983).

11. Ibid., pp. 204–211.

12. A very wise book on the realities of working within the church as institution is David O. Moberg, *The Church as a Social Institution: The Sociology of American Religion* (Prentice–Hall, 1962), though dated in parts and unfortunately out of print. See also Mott, *Biblical Ethics and Social Change*, Part II, "Paths to Justice," and Dieter Hessel, *Social Ministry* (Westminster Press, 1982).

3. Preaching in the Contemporary World / Forbes

1. Idries Shah, *Tales of the Dervishes: Teaching-Stories of the Sufi Masters Over the Past Thousand Years* (London: Jonathan Cape, 1967); cited in Robert E. Ornstein, "Contemporary Sufism," in *Transpersonal Psychologies*, ed. by Charles T. Tart (Harper & Brothers, 1959), pp. 356–357.

4. Proclaiming Liberation for the Earth's Sake / Willis

1. Cf. Jürgen Moltmann, *The Church in the Power of the Spirit* (Harper & Row, 1977), pp. 206ff.

2. Stanley Hauerwas, "On Surviving Justly: An Ethical Analysis of Disarmament," in *Religious Conscience and Nuclear War*, ed. by J. Raitt (University of Missouri Press, 1982), p. 1.

3. Gustavo Gutiérrez, *A Theology of Liberation* (Orbis Books, 1973), p. ix. Cf. also Juan Luis Segundo, *The Sacraments Today* (Orbis Books, 1974), pp. 90ff., on "A Community in Dialogue," and Letty M. Russell, *Human Liberation in a Feminist Perspective* (Westminster Press, 1974), pp. 157ff., on the "open ecclesiology" which seeks participation in God's traditioning activity.

4. Gutiérrez, *A Theology of Liberation*, p. 11.

5. George Lindbeck calls attention to this in a different way in his article, "An Assessment Reassessed: Paul Tillich on the Reformation," *The Journal of Religion*, Oct. 1983, pp. 376–393. Tillich's "Protestant principle" presupposed what he called "Catholic substance," which Lindbeck summarizes as "a total milieu rich in symbolism, mystery, sacraments, and liturgical celebration with a strong sense of tradition and of the wider church community and its authority" (p. 378). Lindbeck writes that "to use a contrast Tillich once employs, the Protestant principle is corrective rather than constitutive of the church. To make it constitutive leads ultimately to the evisceration of Protestantism. The story of later Protestantism from this perspective is that of protracted and progressive disaster. Because of the schism, the continuing polemic with Rome, and internal divisions, the Protestant principle has become constitutive rather than corrective. Gradually the Catholic substance has drained away" (p. 380).

6. Cf. chapter I of The Second Helvetic Confession, in *The Book of Confessions* (The Constitution, Part I; New York and Atlanta: Presbyterian Church (U.S.A.), 1983), 5.004. The Word of God in its threefold form, including preaching, remains an event of the mystery of grace by which the human words are used to bear the good news. Cf. Karl Barth, *Church Dogmatics* I/1, Sec. 4, and Moltmann's qualification of this correct insight in *The Church in the Power of the Spirit*, pp. 207–210.

7. Walter Kasper, *Jesus the Christ* (Paulist Press, 1976), p. 15; and John Knox, *The Church and the Reality of Christ* (Harper & Row, 1962), pp. 13ff.

8. Kasper, *Jesus the Christ*, pp. 245ff. Cf. also D. Willis, "The Material Assumptions of Integrative Theology," *Princeton Seminary Bulletin*, Summer 1979, pp. 232–250, esp. 236ff.; Aloys Grillmeier, *Christ in Christian Tradition* (Sheed & Ward,

1965) on the Cappadocian Christology, pp. 278ff.; and P. Lehmann, *Ideology and Incarnation* (Geneva, 1962), pp. 23ff.

9. Knox, *The Church and the Reality of Christ*, pp. 37ff.

10. That is the significance of adopting a book of confessions with the explicit understanding that an ecclesial community in the confessing tradition makes confessions in subsequent generations and cultures in order to keep confessing the apostolic faith freshly.

11. *The Book of Confessions*, 8.11–15.

12. Cf. Russell, *Human Liberation in a Feminist Perspective*, chapter 3, for a discussion of the search for a usable past; and James Cone, *A Black Theology of Liberation* (J. B. Lippincott, 1970), esp. chapter 4.

13. See Gregory Nazianzus' Letter 101 to Cledonius, in *Enchiridion Patristicum*, coll. M. J. Rouët de Journal (Barcelona, 1959), p. 381.

14. See Augustine, *Confessions* 10.6, in Albert Outler (ed.), *Augustine: Confessions and Enchiridion*, Library of Christian Classics (Westminster Press, 1955), pp. 205–207, and *The City of God* 14.7 and 14.28, in the edition by David Knowles (Penguin Books, 1972), pp. 556–558 and 593f. Cf. Anders Nygren, *Agape and Eros* (Westminster Press, 1953), pp. 476ff.

15. See Luther's Heidelberg Disputation of 1518, in John Dillenberger (ed.), *Martin Luther: Selections from His Writings* (Doubleday & Co., Anchor Books, 1961), pp. 501–503.

16. Cf. Jürgen Moltmann, *The Experiment Hope* (Fortress Press, 1975), esp. chapters 4, 10, and 11; and Roy W. Fairchild, *Finding Hope Again* (Harper & Row, 1980), esp. chapters 3 and 7.

17. James E. Loder, *The Transforming Moment* (Harper & Row, 1981), pp. 29ff.

18. Jürgen Moltmann, *The Crucified God* (Harper & Row, 1974), pp. 227–249.

19. See Tissa Balasuriya, *The Eucharist and Human Liberation* (Orbis Books, 1979), esp. chapters 1 and 10.

6. Process Theology and Eco-Justice / Cauthen

1. References to nearly all these areas can be found in a combination of the following books: Marilyn Ferguson, *The Aquarian Conspiracy* (J. P. Tarcher, 1980); Morris Berman,

The Reenchantment of the World (Cornell University Press, 1981); Ludwig von Bertalanffy, *General System Theory* (George Braziller, 1969); David Bohm, *Wholeness and the Implicate Order* (London: Routledge & Kegan Paul, 1972); L. C. Birch and John Cobb, *The Liberation of Life* (Cambridge University Press, 1981); Herman E. Daly (ed.), *Toward a Steady-State Economy* (W. H. Freeman & Co., 1973); Huston Smith, *Beyond the Post-Modern Mind* (Crossroad Publishing Co., 1982); Frederick Ferré, *Shaping the Future* (Harper & Row, 1976); George Cabot Lodge, *The New American Ideology* (Alfred A. Knopf, 1975), and William Ophuls, *Ecology and the Politics of Scarcity* (W. H. Freeman & Co., 1977).

2. The literature of process theology is enormous and growing. A brief introduction with an extensive annotated bibliography can be found in John Cobb and David Griffin, *Process Theology: An Introductory Exposition* (Westminster Press, 1976).

3. This is Whitehead's own description of his point of view in the preface to *Process and Reality* (Macmillan Co., 1929), p. v.

4. A classic statement is Alfred North Whitehead, *Science and the Modern World* (Macmillan Co., 1925). See also Kenneth Cauthen, *Science, Secularization and God* (Abingdon Press, 1969).

5. Kenneth Cauthen, *Christian Biopolitics* (Abingdon Press, 1971), p. 106.

6. Whitehead, *Process and Reality*, p. viii.

7. See Cobb and Griffin, *Process Theology*, pp. 63–79.

8. Alfred North Whitehead, *The Function of Reason* (Princeton University Press, 1929), p. 10.

9. I have developed this theory of ethics, along with a theory of justice, in a full-length book, *Process Ethics: A Constructive System* (Edwin Mellen Press, 1984). Also see my *The Ethics of Enjoyment* (John Knox Press, 1975).

10. A full consideration of the complexities of justice on this score would require definitions of and distinctions among at least the following: the good of the whole, the common good, total good, the good of groups, and the good of individuals.

7. Eco-Justice Themes in Christian Ethics / Shinn

1. William Temple, *Nature, Man and God* (London: Macmillan & Co., 1949), p. 478.

2. Lynn White, Jr., "The Historical Roots of Our Ecologic Crisis," *Science* 155 (March 10, 1967): 1205.

3. René Dubos, *A God Within* (Charles Scribner's Sons, 1972), p. 168.

4. Aristotle, *Politics*, 1256b, 20–26.

5. J. Donald Hughes, *Ecology in Ancient Civilizations* (University of New Mexico Press, 1975), p. 149.

6. E. F. Schumacher, an address to the British Council of Churches, April 28, 1971. I am using a text circulated to the Working Group on Church and Society, World Council of Churches.

7. Walt W. Rostow, *The Stages of Economic Growth* (Cambridge University Press, 1960).

8. John Kenneth Galbraith, *The Affluent Society* (Houghton Mifflin Co., 1958).

9. For a fuller discussion of this issue, see Roger L. Shinn, "The End of a Liberal Dream," *Christianity and Crisis* 41 (March 16, 1981): 52–57.

10. Joseph Sittler, "Called to Unity," *Ecumenical Review* 14, no. 2 (Jan. 1962), 186, 188.

11. Kenneth E. Boulding, "The Wisdom of God and the Wisdom of Man," in *Human Values on the Spaceship Earth* (New York: National Council of Churches, 1966).

12. William and Paul Paddock, *Famine—1975! America's Decision: Who Will Survive?* (Little, Brown & Co., 1967).

13. Garrett Hardin, "Lifeboat Ethics: The Case Against Helping the Poor," *Psychology Today*, Sept. 1974.

14. Frances Moore Lappé and Joseph Collins, *Food First: Beyond the Myth of Scarcity* (Houghton Mifflin Co., 1977).

15. V. I. Lenin, "The Tasks of the Youth Leagues" (1920) quoted by Langdon Winner, *Autonomous Technology: Technics-out-of-Control as a Theme in Political Thought* (MIT Press, 1977), p. 267.

16. See Donella Meadows, "Limits to Growth Revisited," in *Finite Resources and the Human Future*, ed. by Ian G. Barbour (Augsburg Publishing House, 1976). Address at a symposium at Carleton College, Oct. 3–5, 1975. My report includes unpublished remarks made publicly at the symposium.

17. OPEC oil prices at the Persian Gulf were $1.00–$1.20 per barrel in 1969, $34 per barrel in 1981. See *Energy Future: Report of the Energy Project at the Harvard Business School*, ed. by

Robert Stobaugh and Daniel Yergin (Random House, 1979), p. 25.

18. UPI dispatch, reporting on a study by Dr. James F. Fries of Stanford University Medical Center in the *New England Journal of Medicine; New York Times,* July 18, 1980, p. A6.

19. Nick Eberstadt, "Myths of the Food Crisis," *New York Review of Books,* Feb. 19, 1976, p. 34.

20. William K. Stevens, "India's 'Forced March' to Modernity," *New York Times Magazine,* Jan. 22, 1984, p. 28.

21. Barry Commoner, *The Closing Circle* (Alfred A. Knopf, 1972), pp. 41–45.

8. Preaching for Creation's Sake / Hessel

1. Robert Bellah, *The Broken Covenant: American Civil Religion in Time of Trial* (Seabury Press, 1975), p. 1; and Kenneth Cauthen, *The Ethics of Enjoyment* (John Knox Press, 1975), p. 40 and chapter 3.

2. Nicholas Wolterstorff, *Until Justice and Peace Embrace* (Wm. B. Eerdmans Publishing Co., 1983), p. 56.

3. Discussed by Norman Gottwald in chapter 2.

4. Roger L. Shinn, *Forced Options: Social Decisions for the 21st Century* (Harper & Row, 1982).

5. *A Statement on Acid Rain* is one of several recent theologically articulate statements by North American ecumenical gatherings in response to the eco-justice crisis. It is available from the National Council of Churches, 475 Riverside Dr., Room 572, New York, NY 10115, or from the United Church of Canada, 85 St. Clair Ave. E., Toronto, Ontario M4T 1M8.

6. Phyllis Trible, *God and the Rhetoric of Sexuality* (Fortress Press, 1978), chapters 3 and 4. Also see Dorothee Soelle, *To Work and to Love: A Theology of Creation* (Fortress Press, 1984), chapters 1–5.

7. Wolterstorff, p. 124.

8. Discussed by William E. Gibson in chapter 1.

9. Wolterstorff, pp. 64, 67.

10. Discussed by Norman Gottwald in chapter 2.

11. Wolterstorff, p. 85.

12. Douglas John Hall, *The Steward: A Biblical Symbol Come of Age* (Friendship Press, 1983), pp. 55, 99f.

13. Discussed by E. David Willis in chapter 4.

14. Isabel Carter Heyward, *The Redemption of God* (University Press of America, 1982), p. 183.
15. See Dieter T. Hessel (ed.), *Social Themes of the Christian Year* (Geneva Press, 1983), for examples.
16. Denominations and organizations that relate to the National Council of the Churches of Christ in the U.S.A., Division of Church and Society, have formed an Eco-Justice Working Group. It provides churches and secular groups selected educational resources, issue analysis, and action suggestions in the arena where concerns for ecological sustainability and distributive justice intersect. The Working Group responds to specific issues of hazardous wastes, air pollution, and energy policy. For information, contact Director of Economic Justice, NCC-DCS, Room 572, 475 Riverside Drive, New York, NY 10115

Selected Readings

Balasuriya, Tissa. *The Eucharist and Human Liberation*. Orbis Books, 1979.

Barbour, Ian G., ed. *Earth Might Be Fair*. Prentice-Hall, 1972.

———. *Technology, Environment, and Human Values*. Praeger Publishers, 1980.

Belo, Fernando. *A Materialist Reading of the Gospel of Mark*. Orbis Books, 1981.

Birch, Bruce C., and Larry L. Rasmussen. *Bible and Ethics in the Christian Life*. Augsburg Publishing House, 1976.

———. *The Predicament of the Prosperous*. Westminster Press, 1978.

Birch, L. C., and John B. Cobb, Jr. *The Liberation of Life*. Cambridge University Press, 1981.

Brown, Delwin. *To Set at Liberty*. Orbis Books, 1980.

Brown, Lester R. *The State of the World, 1985: A Worldwatch Institute Report on Progress Toward a Sustainable Society*. W. W. Norton & Co., 1985.

———. *The Twenty-Ninth Day*. W. W. Norton & Co., 1978.

Capra, Fritjof. *The Tao of Physics: An Exploration of the Parallels Between Modern Physics and Eastern Mysticism*. Shambhala Publications, 1975.

———. *The Turning Point: Science, Society and the Rising Culture*. Simon & Schuster, 1962; Bantam Books, 1983.

Cauthen, Kenneth. *The Ethics of Enjoyment*. John Knox Press, 1975.

———. *Process Ethics: A Constructive System*. Edwin Mellen Press, 1984.

Cobb, John B., Jr. *Process Theology as Political Theology*. Westminster Press, 1982.

———— and W. Widick Schroeder, eds. *Process Philosophy and Social Thought.* Center for the Scientific Study of Religion, 1981.

Daly, Herman E., ed. *Economics, Ecology, Ethics: Essays Toward a Steady-State Economy.* W. H. Freeman & Co., 1980.

Derr, Thomas Sieger. *Ecology and Human Need.* Westminster Press, 1975.

Devaney, Sheila Greeve, ed. *Feminism and Process Thought.* Edwin Mellen Press, 1981.

Fairchild, Roy W. *Finding Hope Again: A Pastor's Guide to Counseling Depressed Persons.* Harper & Row, 1980.

Ferkiss, Victor. *The Future of Technological Civilization.* George Braziller, 1974.

Gibson, William E. *A Covenant Group for Lifestyle Assessment.* Rev. ed. New York: Program Agency, United Presbyterian Church U.S.A., 1981.

The Global 2000 Report to the President: Entering the Twenty-first Century. A report prepared by the Council on Environmental Quality and the Department of State. U.S. Government Printing Office, 1980. Vol. I summarizes the report; vols. II and III provide technical data.

Gottwald, Norman K., ed. *The Bible and Liberation: Political and Social Hermeneutics.* Orbis Books, 1983.

Gray, Elizabeth Dodson. *Green Paradise Lost.* Roundtable Press, 1979.

————. *Patriarchy as a Conceptual Trap.* Roundtable Press, 1982.

Gregorios, Paulos. *The Human Presence: An Orthodox View of Nature.* Geneva: World Council of Churches, 1978.

Griffin, David R., and John B. Cobb, Jr., eds. *Mind in Nature: Essays on the Interface of Science and Philosophy.* University Press of America, 1977.

Hall, Douglas John. *The Steward: A Biblical Symbol Come of Age.* Friendship Press, 1983.

Hart, John. *The Spirit of the Earth: A Theory of the Land.* Paulist Press, 1984.

Haught, John F. *Nature and Purpose.* University Press of America, 1980.

Heilbroner, Robert L. *An Inquiry Into the Human Prospect.* Rev. ed. W. W. Norton & Co., 1980.

Hessel, Dieter T., ed. *Energy Ethics: A Christian Response.* Friendship Press, 1979.

————. *Social Themes of the Christian Year: A Commentary on the Lectionary.* Geneva Press, 1983.

Hirsch, Fred. *Social Limits to Growth.* Harvard University Press, 1976.

Hughes, J. Donald. *Ecology in Ancient Civilizations.* University of New Mexico Press, 1975.

Joranson, Philip N., and Ken Butigan, eds. *Cry of the Environment.* Bear & Co., 1984.

Kasper, Walter. *Jesus the Christ.* Paulist Press, 1976.

Lehmann, Paul. *The Transfiguration of Politics.* Harper & Row, 1975.

Loder, James E. *The Transforming Moment: Understanding Convictional Experiences.* Harper & Row, 1981.

Meadows, Donella H., et al. *The Limits to Growth: A Report for the Club of Rome's Project on the Predicament of Mankind.* Universe Books, 1972.

Moltmann, Jürgen. *The Church in the Power of the Spirit.* Harper & Row, 1977.

Mott, Stephen Charles. *Biblical Ethics and Social Change.* Oxford University Press, 1982.

Ogden, Schubert. *Faith and Freedom.* Abingdon Press, 1979.

Ogletree, Thomas W. *The Use of the Bible in Christian Ethics.* Fortress Press, 1983.

Ophuls, William. *Ecology and the Politics of Scarcity: Prologue to a Political Theory of the Steady State.* W. H. Freeman & Co., 1977.

Rifkin, Jeremy, with Ted Howard. *The Emerging Order: God in the Age of Scarcity.* G. P. Putnam's Sons, 1979.

Rosaldo, Michelle Zimbalist, and Louise Lamphere, eds. *Woman, Culture and Society.* Stanford University Press, 1974.

Sagan, Carl. *Cosmos.* Random House, 1980.

Schumacher, E. F. *Small Is Beautiful: Economics as if People Mattered.* Harper & Row, 1973.

Shinn, Roger L. *Forced Options: Social Decisions for the 21st Century.* Harper & Row, 1982.

————, ed. *Faith and Science in an Unjust World: Report of the World Council of Churches Conference on Faith, Science and the Future.* Vol. I, Papers. Geneva: World Council of Churches, 1980.

Soelle, Dorothee, and Shirley A. Cloyes. *To Work and to Love: A Theology of Creation.* Fortress Press, 1984.

Swartley, Willard M. *Slavery, Sabbath, War and Women: Case Issues in Biblical Interpretation.* Herald Press, 1983.

Wilkinson, Loren, ed. *Earthkeeping: Christian Stewardship of Natural Resources*. 2nd ed. Wm. B. Eerdmans Publishing Co., 1980.

Wolterstorff, Nicholas. *Until Justice and Peace Embrace*. Wm. B. Eerdmans Publishing Co., 1983.